Handmade Beginnings

24 Sewing Projects to Welcome Baby

by Anna Maria Horner

WILEY

Wiley Publishing, Inc.

Acquisitions Editor
Roxane Cerda

Project Editor
Donna Wright

Editorial Manager
Christina Stambaugh

Publisher
Cindy Kitchel

Vice President and
Executive Publisher
Kathy Nebenhaus

Interior Design
Tai Blanche

Page Layout
Erin Zeltner

Graphics Technicians
Rhonda David-Burroughs
Brent Savage
Rashell Smith

Cover Design
Susan Olinsky

Photography
Angela Crutcher

For general information on our other products and services or to obtain technical support please contact our Customer Care Department within the U.S. at (877) 762-2974, outside the U.S. at (317) 572-3993 or fax (317) 572-4002.

Wiley also publishes its books in a variety of electronic formats. Some content that appears in print may not be available in electronic books. For more information about Wiley products, please visit our web site at www.wiley.com.

Library of Congress Cataloging-in-Publication data

Horner, Anna Maria, 1972-
  Handmade beginnings : 24 sewing projects to welcome baby / by Anna Maria Horner.
     p. cm.
  Includes bibliographical references.
  ISBN-13: 978-0-470-49781-4
  ISBN-10: 0-470-49781-5
  1. Sewing. 2. Infants' supplies. 3. Nurseries--Equipment and supplies. 4. Maternity clothes. I. Title.
  TT705.H83 1998
  646.4'06--dc22

                                              2010002931

Printed in China

10 9 8 7 6 5 4 3 2 1

Book production by Wiley Publishing, Inc., Composition Services

Anna Maria's original patterns are intended for non-commercial, personal use only and not to be used in the production of goods for sale in any quantity.

*This book is dedicated with love and
a million thank yous to my husband, Jeff.
Our family is built upon your love,
and so are all of my dreams.*

Acknowledgments

I'd like to thank the following beautiful women, moms, dads, and children for their willingness to lend themselves and their joy to help make the photographs in this book both inspiring and real: Angela Nelms, Claire Nelms, Christina Changas, Allie Murphy, Marios Gerasimopoulos, Carrie Gontarek, Reuben Allen, Joseph Horner, Nicolas Horner, Eleni Horner, Isabela Horner, Jeff Horner, Juliana Horner, Roman Horner, and Katherine Darsinos.

Working with Angela Crutcher on the book photography was both a blessing and an adventure. I'd like to thank Angela for her willingness to collaborate and her natural ability to bring out the inner beauty in every little person she meets.

I'd also like to thank my children, Juliana, Nicolas, Joseph, Isabela, and Eleni, for helping each other and helping me through the welcoming and care of their brother, Roman. Every one of you has made mothering a sixth baby and authoring a second book a joyous possibility. I love each of you dearly.

Table of Contents

Introduction

Every family has a story. Each time we've welcomed a new baby, the story of our own family has a new beginning. Our children have brought more than their own chapter to our story, but they have, in fact, rewritten the rest of us. The whole family, together and individually, is remade into something it wasn't before—something we wouldn't have ever guessed or expected.

I have always felt compelled during my pregnancies to make items for the new one. Similar to the quintessential image of an expectant mother working away with her knitting needles on a pair of baby booties, I set out to stack fabrics and ideas in high piles that I can work through as my belly grows. Perhaps it's just the typical nesting that all mothers go through, or maybe its nervous energy. Whatever the explanation, answering the desire to create as I await a new baby seems to be my own way of nurturing.

What has taken me precisely six children and countless handmade items to realize, is that this sewing, or *nurturing,* which is intended mostly for the baby or our home, perhaps benefits me more than anyone in the family. Slow hand-stitching forces me off my tired feet and allows me to pay attention to the subtle bumps and squirms of the little one within. Running my hands over potential fabrics for the baby's clothing to check for softness sets my mind into daydreams of what color eyes or hair the baby might have. Using what brain power is still available to me while pregnant, I ponder the design of a nursery quilt which gives me less time to ponder those natural fears and doubts that come with motherhood. All this to say, sewing while expecting has kept me healthy and centered on what matters—more joyful than not. It goes without saying too, that all this sewing has outfitted our babies, beds, toy shelves, and home with beautiful items that are well loved and often tucked away for safekeeping.

While most of my experiences with sewing to welcome a baby involve being the mama, this book does not ignore everyone else in the baby's life! Dads, brothers, sisters, adoptive moms, foster moms, and all . . . this book and its projects are for you too! I hope that the ideas I've sewn and written here inspire the work of your hands and the work of your heart. And I hope that you continue to reach for this book every time to you hear the good news of a baby on the way.

XO

Anna Maria

CHAPTER

1

Baby Steps

Perhaps the new baby in your life came as a complete surprise. Or maybe you've scheduled the beginning of your family down to the hour of arrival. The anticipation and joy of a new life beginning is the same, no matter the amount of planning that took place. With your sewing projects, however, a few pointers and a little forethought will help get you started.

This small chapter should answer some of the questions you may have as you head into each of the sewing projects. A chapter orientation, pattern making tips, sizing guides, basic tools, and fabric selection advice are all covered here, so take a few minutes to give this chapter at least a skim before beginning your sewing. And if you're expecting, get a glass of milk and put your feet up while doing so, please.

Sewing for Mama, Baby, Family, and Nest

The four following sewing chapters, and the items found in each, are designed to include all that will welcome a baby home. The projects in each chapter are ordered from ideal for beginners to ideal for experienced sewers. So the first project in each chapter is generally the simplest to sew, and the last project generally requires more advanced skills. In some cases, the time involvement alone is what lends a given project to being ranked as more advanced. So if you're a beginner, there are plenty of projects that you can take on with confidence, and within each chapter you might try working through them in sequence.

Mama Sewing

As the Mama of many, I personally like the idea of thinking of Mama first! But truly, welcoming a new baby should always begin by taking very good care of the one who will first "house" the little one. It's a real treat for an expectant mom to receive gifts that are for her and her alone, long before the baby even arrives. The Mama Sewing projects are designed to transition with a pregnant woman from the beginning all the way to becoming a nursing mom. The added beauty of each and every Mama project is that you don't have to be pregnant or breastfeeding to make or use any of these stylish items. Each maternity garment project describes modifications that allow you to sew the same item into a non-maternity version. So have fun with them whether you're an expectant mom, an auntie, a granny, an adoptive mommy, or you just love gorgeous handmade clothing and accessories.

The sizing guide below will be helpful when you are making garments for Mama. This guide gives actual body measurements, and each of the projects will give finished garment dimensions for each size. So between the two, you will be able to determine which size to make. The maternity items account for growth in just about all areas, so use pre-pregnancy measurements (or very early pregnancy measurements) to find the right size. When measuring the bust and hips, be sure to measure around at a level line at the fullest point of the bust and hips. When measuring the waistline, be sure to keep the measuring tape level around the belly button.

Mama Sizes			
Size	Bust	Natural Waist	Hips
Small (S)	34/35"	27/28"	36/37"
Medium (M)	36/37"	29/30"	38/39"
Large (L)	38/39"	31/32"	40/41"

If the finished garment dimensions listed with a given project seem way too big, it's likely that your bust and belly will grow into them in not too much time. Your desired length won't change too much for skirts, dresses, and tunics; however, the larger your belly grows, the shorter the front of these garments will become. So keep this in mind if they seem too long in the front when you're sewing early in your pregnancy.

Also, there are always some maternity items that won't last through the entire pregnancy, so don't worry if something you make suddenly doesn't fit when you're a few weeks away from delivering. I've designed these patterns so that favorite garments can be remade into non-maternity items after the baby.

Baby Sewing

Naturally, right after Mama, we must prepare for the precious little show stealer. The projects in the Baby Sewing chapter run the gamut from irresistibly cute to incredibly convenient. With the exception of the Pretty-as-a-Picture Dress, each Baby project is just as darling for a boy as it is for a girl, so a simple fabric switch is all you need to customize your sewing. These Baby sewing projects were inspired by years of clothing my children in basic pieces. Experienced moms know that most babies are happiest wearing nothing at all. However adorable that is, when practicality demands it, we also know that simple and sweet pieces (plus a zillion Onesies) go a long way to keeping baby stylish and comfortable. The baby garment sizes are offered from 0–3 months all the way up to 24 months, so you can make several versions of your favorite patterns ahead of time as you plan for changing seasons and a growing baby.

The Baby Sizing guide below will help you determine which sizes to make for your little one. There are also finished

dimensions listed with each of the baby projects. When sewing for someone else's baby, consider the season that it will be once the baby would be wearing that particular size. It's always a bummer if someone gives you a gorgeous handmade winter jacket, but it fits baby perfectly in the middle of hot and sunny July. Most babies, unless they were premature or otherwise petite, are wearing the next size grouping about a month or so ahead of time. So if you are sewing something for a 2½-month-old that is in season to wear now, you would want to make a 3–6 month size. And if you're making something for a season or two ahead and are not sure how big the baby will have grown by then, it's always best to err on the side of a larger size rather than a smaller size. You can always ask what size the baby is currently wearing, and there is definitely no harm in asking to drop by and measure the little munchkin, either.

Family Sewing

That baby didn't get here all by itself, and in addition to Dad, perhaps there are already one or more eager siblings at home waiting for the new baby to arrive. The Family Sewing chapter is written with the entire household in mind, whether this is your first baby or your tenth baby. Some of the more time-consuming projects are designed for longevity, and they will no doubt become special family heirlooms that mark these all-too-quick and beautiful days in your lives together. Some projects, such as the Patchwork Welcome Notes and Swaddled Baby Love, are wonderful ways to include your older children in all the baby fuss. When making gifts for an expectant family, it is always such a thoughtful gesture to remember the older siblings. And keeping them occupied is never a bad idea.

Baby Sizes						
Body Measurements	3 Months	6 Months	9 Months	12 Months	18 Months	24 Months
Chest	18"	19"	19½"	20"	20½"	21"
Hip	19"	20"	20½"	21"	21½"	22"
Head to Heel	23"	26"	27½"	29"	30½"	32"
Side Waist to Foot	11¼"	13½"	14⅝"	15¾"	16⅞"	18"

Nest Sewing

Settling your baby into the family nest might mean setting up a corner in the master bedroom, carving some space out of an older sibling's room, or creating a little universe that belongs completely to the baby. In any case, sewing and decorating for your new addition is one of the most rewarding ways to spend those seemingly endless days of waiting for the big arrival. The projects in the Nest Sewing chapter are designed to both comfort and delight the little one, but are not so shortsighted that they won't also grow beautifully with your baby into a bigger kid room.

How to Use the Patterns

Many sewing projects in this book have corresponding patterns on one or more of the seven fold-in pattern pages that are included in the book's envelope pocket. If a project has a corresponding pattern, it will list the pattern page in the materials list at the beginning of the project.

In order to provide several full-size original patterns all in one book, the pattern pieces overlap one another and therefore will first need to be traced using tracing paper. If a project has several sizes, the line styles that each size is drawn with will vary and will be labeled to help you follow the correct size as you trace. Some pattern pieces will have a common line that all of the sizes will follow. And further, the pattern pages are printed in two colors to help differentiate pattern pieces from one another. Once the pattern lines are traced, you'll need to also trace any of the markings, such as button placement, notches, and so on from the pattern onto your pattern tracing. The traced pattern can then be cut out

with craft scissors and used to cut the fabric and begin your sewing.

Just a few of the pattern pieces have "continued" in their titles, meaning the project instructions will ask you to first join two pattern pieces together with tape (or trace together on the tracing paper) to create the full pattern piece before beginning the fabric cutting.

Many of the projects have no need for patterns and just describe the more simplistic pattern pieces in dimension only. You can either cut directly from the fabric when making these items, or choose to go ahead and make some labeled tracing paper patterns as you go so that you can easily make the item again in the future.

All patterns provided on the pattern pages and those patterns that are described in dimension have seam allowances included, so there is no need to add any. Seam allowance depths will vary from one project to another and will also vary within each project, so pay special attention as you read project instructions.

Yardage requirements mentioned in the materials list generally are considered for 44/45-inch wide fabrics. Therefore, wider fabrics might require less yardage.

As with every sewing pattern, it's always a good idea to read through the entire set of instructions, also paying attention to the illustrations, before you even begin to cut the pattern pieces out of fabric. Often a step will seem confusing until you read a little further through the next few steps, and then suddenly it'll click. Below is a key to the figure illustrations denoting fabric right side, wrong side, and interfacings/fusibles.

Right side

Wrong side

Interfacing

Sewing Tools

Because so many of the projects will require the same basic tools, the following section is an overview of those tools. These basic go-to tools will therefore not be listed at the beginning of every project, but the materials list for each project will generally include the actual materials that will compose the item you are making.

Tracing Paper or Semi-Translucent Craft Paper

A 24-inch-wide roll of tracing paper is really useful in conjunction with the patterns in this book, as well as many of your other craft projects. These rolls are generally available at most large art supply stores and online. A quality craft paper or vellum that you can see through enough for tracing also works well and will be more durable for those patterns that you'd like to save and sew with several times. Try Plaza Artist Materials & Picture Framing to order online at www.plazaart.com, or look for a location in your neighborhood.

Making Notes to Yourself

In addition to using simple pens, pencils, and erasers to perfect your paper patterns, you'll want to have a healthy supply of water-soluble fabric pens and fabric chalk pencils for marking pattern notes, such as button placement and so on, directly onto the fabric. Particularly with the embroidery projects, having a water-soluble fabric pen that you've tested and are comfortable with is very helpful. Once I'm finished with a project and want to fade out the pen lines, I use a small, clean paintbrush with a little water on it to gently brush away the marks. This way, I don't have to immerse or wash the item completely. While you could also use the mist of a water bottle, a paintbrush is more precise. All of these items are readily available at your local craft/fabric store.

Template Plastic

Quilt template plastic for tracing patterns is a very useful item to have for small pattern shapes that you will cut repeatedly and want to save. It cuts easily with scissors or a craft knife and won't curl like most types of paper will once they are cut

into smaller shapes. I recommend using template plastic to create the pattern pieces for both the Center of Attention Quilt and the Scrappy Nap Pillow. This is also easily found at your local quilt shop.

Cotton Muslin

Having a bolt or two of inexpensive muslin in your sewing studio makes you a clever crafter. Usually just a couple of dollars per yard, this versatile fabric is an ideal way to test a garment's size, or to perfect your quilt piecing style without cutting into your favorite, more expensive fabrics. Because most varieties of muslin are somewhat sheer, you could also trace a pattern right onto the muslin to test-fit a size before you even create a paper pattern. Several of the projects in the book, particularly the embroidery projects, use muslin as a background fabric, so get at least a few yards to begin with anyway.

Cutting and Measuring Tools

Without a doubt, having at least three types of scissors at your side is extremely helpful. Craft scissors are useful for cutting out the patterns from tracing paper and template plastic. Dressmaking scissors are suitable for all large fabric cutting. And some small scissors or thread snips are great to clip threads, both at the sewing machine and as you sit with hand sewing in your lap.

A rotary blade combined with a clear quilt ruler and cutting mat creates a perfect set of tools for measuring and cutting basic squares and rectangles. A cutting mat and a large, clear, plastic quilt ruler can also help in marking off lines, and trimming fabrics to get the edges clean and "square."

I boast an unhealthy number of clear, plastic quilt rulers in almost every size and shape; however, I continue to reach for these three quite frequently:

- 8-x-24-inch grid
- 3½-x-18½-inch grid
- 60-degree triangular ruler (used in the Sixth Time's the Charm Crib Quilt project on page 151)

With one or more of these and a large cutting mat, you'll seldom have any use for a standard ruler or yardstick.

Ironing Tools

A steam iron and ironing board are imperative for almost every project in this book. It's also good to have a pressing cloth around to protect fine fabrics, and any laminated fabrics you may choose to sew with. Pressing hams are helpful, but I find a rolled-up hand towel more versatile. I have even appropriated a hair straightener to press the tiniest of the Nesting Cubes in order to fuse the interfacing into areas that I can't reach with the iron. Always follow the manufacturer's directions for both fabrics and fusibles for the appropriate heat setting, and test a corner first.

Needle and Thread Assortment

For the machine-sewing projects, all of the recommended fabrics are woven, so a universal needle type in a small range of sizes, from 11 to 16 or so, will be all you need to complete your sewing. I recommend Coats Dual Duty XP thread for all projects except for the quilting projects, where I would recommend 100-percent Coats Cotton thread for the machine piecing. The thread recommendations for all hand-sewing steps are the same, and some simple hand-sewing needles, or "sharps," will suffice.

For embroidery and hand quilting, I keep several sizes of embroidery needles on hand because they are nice and sharp and have a large eye that makes threading thicker threads easier. For embroidery and hand-quilting stitches, I personally go back and forth between several types of six-strand cotton floss and quilting thread, such as DMC's embroidery floss and DMC's Perle Cottons. In general, I choose them based on a specific texture that I'm looking for to enhance the feel of a given project; therefore, use your own best judgment when choosing floss and threads. Having a full spectrum of colors inspires your work a lot more than just a handful, so I do recommend splurging on your color range!

Fabrics
Fabrics for Mama

Choosing fabric for your maternity items is really no different than choosing fabric for any garment sewing, but you may want to keep just a few things in mind to make the most of your time with thread and needle. When you are pregnant, your wardrobe typically shrinks considerably in numbers of outfits. Because of this, you'll want each piece that you sew to be as versatile as possible. You may therefore choose colors and prints that are easily mixed in with the rest of your wearable wardrobe so that you can really get some mileage out of a few pieces. For instance, make at least a few items in basic black, charcoal, or some other interesting solids. Let further interest come in by way of accessories, sweaters, scarves, textured tights, and boots—none of which have to be maternity for you to wear. Then, of course, for other maternity pieces, you'll have a bit of fun playing with colors and prints, keeping in mind the hues that flatter your coloring and a scale of print that flatters your blossoming figure.

As far as fabric types go, unless you are specifically sewing for a special occasion, it might be a good idea to keep the fabric content versatile in terms of dressiness. How many times will you be able to wear a silk chiffon tunic over the next 6–9 months? Exactly. Just like sewing for baby, consider the months during which you'll be pregnant and which seasons they will cover in order to choose appropriate fabric weights. More important than perhaps anything is to choose fabrics that feel good to wear. This is no time to willingly add discomfort to your list of emotions.

Whether garments, quilts, or soft toys, as long as the item you are making will continue to be washed after use, it's a good idea to gently wash all fabric in cold water with a mild detergent and drip dry or lightly machine dry before you cut the material into pattern pieces. This will preshrink the fabric so that your sewing in a specific size will remain accurate after the first wear. Prewashing also helps to remove the sizing, or fabric finish, that might have been applied to the material during the manufacturing process. Also press your materials well before beginning your sewing projects.

Fabrics for Baby

I don't think that I'm alone in the comfort that I take knowing my baby is dressed or wrapped in something incredibly soft and comfortable. Breathable fabrics, such as cotton, are ideal for babies, because of their softness and their easy care. When you need to make items that are pretty sturdy and intended for warmth, such as booties and jackets, lining them with 100-percent cotton flannel is a great choice. When making dresses and blouses for your baby girl with a lot of tucks and gathers, nothing beats butter-soft cotton voile to make sweet little details even sweeter. If the fabric is slightly sheer, simply layer the garment over a body suit and tights. You can also temporarily baste two layers of lightweight fabrics together and treat them as one when you follow the sewing pattern instructions, and then remove the basting stitches after the sewing is complete.

Choosing colors for baby isn't too different than choosing colors for anyone based on their coloring and skin tone. There are many baby-style prints out there, but don't lock yourself into juvenile style prints just because you are sewing for a little one. Keeping the palette sophisticated and the print styles top shelf has some really charming results when making baby's wardrobe. So just because a print looks grown up, or is large in scale, don't underestimate the interesting and playful effect of combining those features with a miniature garment. On the opposite end of advice for baby fabrics, keep a sense of humor with you as you combine colors and prints. Don't only choose completely harmonious groups of prints. Have fun. It goes together if you say so—a phrase you're likely to repeat now that you're a parent.

Growing and Sewing

Read even a few paragraphs about newborn development and you'll learn that high-contrast colors and graphic prints help a newborn baby to develop their vision, learn focus, and captivate their attention. Even at 3 months and beyond, exciting colors and prints can entertain a baby for a long while and set their little arms and legs into perpetual motion. Once they begin to feel around for other clues about the world, also at around 3 months old, giving them several different textures to feel and grasp helps to develop their tactile senses. Planning for this stage of baby development is so enjoyable when choosing fabrics for a play quilt, toys, and other nursery accessories, so have fun.

Safety Considerations

In every instance possible, always opt for the safest materials to sew on to your baby's clothing. Little items, such as buttons and trims, should be sewn on to clothing with extra care to ensure safety. Loops and dangling strings or ribbons should be secure and very short in length, no more than a few inches. Drawstrings are not a great feature for baby clothing, nor is any feature or trim that can come undone easily as baby plays in bed before sleeping. Buttons and all such trims should be checked each time you do the wash to be sure they are sewn on securely. Always better safe than sorry, so avoid putting baby to bed or out of your sight wearing clothing that has any of these types of details that can come loose, especially those that are close to the baby's face.

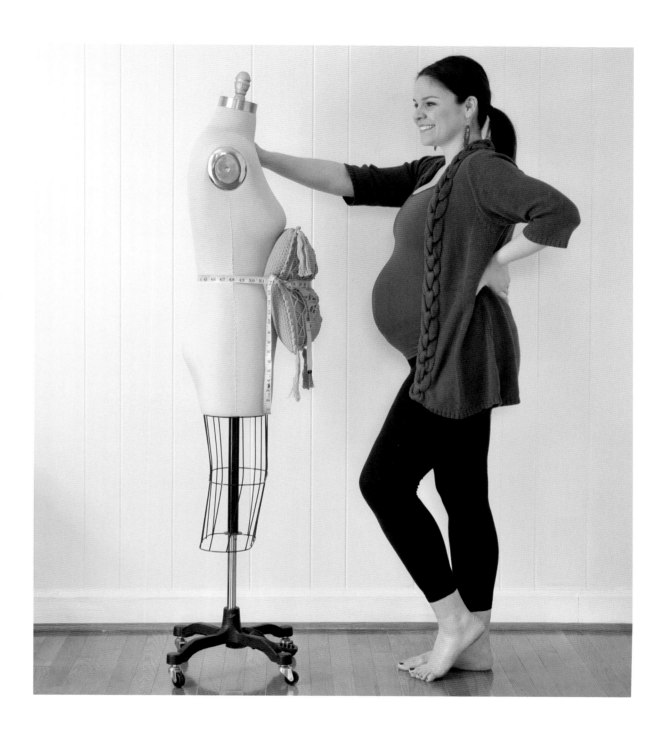

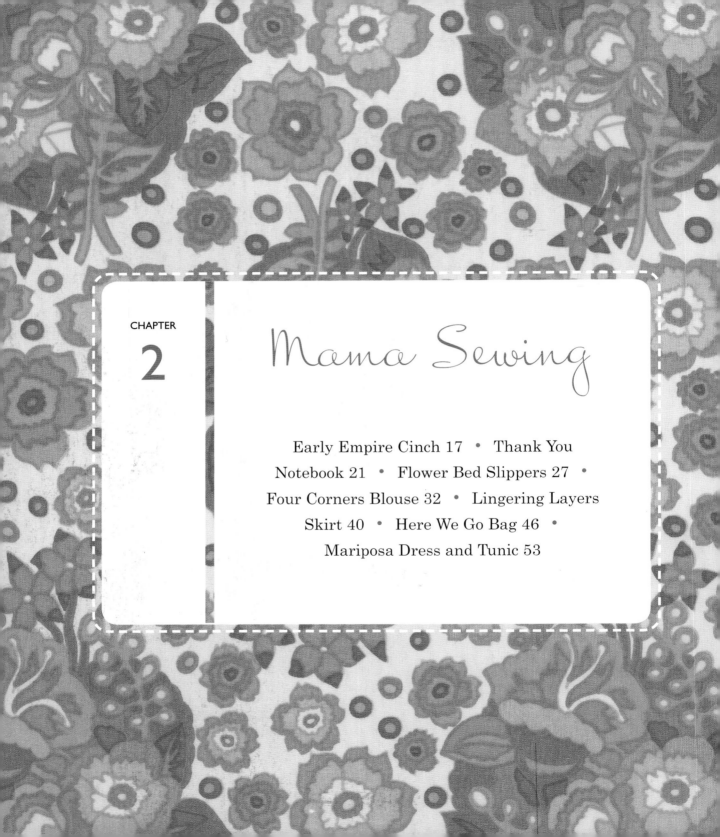

-Early Empire Cinch-

Early Empire Cinch

*T*his empire-waist belt will help give away the secret of your impending arrival (although you don't have to be expecting to enjoy this accessory). Early in pregnancy, a woman's figure often just appears thicker before the noticeable swell of life appears as a round belly. So wearing the wide part of the belt in front, and tying it in back, takes advantage of the room you still have above your belly, and flatters your changing shape. As baby begins to fill out your belly, you can turn the ties to the front and wear the thicker part at your back for a perfectly pregnant silhouette. In either case, this little accessory can transform any maxi dress or blousy blouse into something gorgeously fitted for you. And by making it patchwork on one side and solid on the other, you can have two belts in one.

Materials

Light- to medium-weight woven fabric:
- fabric scraps of various sorts for the patchwork side
- ¼ yard for the solid side

¾ yard of very lightweight woven fabric for edging and ties

At least 6" × 30" of light- to medium-weight interfacing

Early Empire Cinch pattern piece inside the pocket

Finished Dimensions (not including ties):
Small 3" × 25" **Medium** 3" × 27" **Large** 3" × 29"

My Color Notes

For Angela's patchwork cinch, we used several small scraps of vintage kimono fabrics mostly made from silk and silk blends. The result is rich and luxurious, but quirky enough to wear very formal or very casual.

Trace and Cut

1 Trace and cut the Early Empire Cinch piece (**A**) on pattern page 2 in your desired size. Using pattern **A,** cut one from the light- to medium-weight woven fabric on the fabric fold for the Cinch Back, and cut one on the fold from the interfacing.

NOTE: You will need to use pattern piece A once again for the Cinch Front once you've created the patchwork.

2 To create the patchwork side of your Cinch, start by cutting about 30 small strips of various fabrics that are 1½" wide and 4" long, and set aside. (Feel free to cut any style of patchwork pieces you want here.)

3 Cut out bias strips from the edging fabric that measure 1¾" wide. Once joined, you will need a total length of about 60" of bias for the Cinch edging.

4 Cut out two strips for the ties that each measure 3¾" wide and 42" long. (You can modify the ties' length however you wish.)

Assemble the Cinch

5 Arrange and rearrange the patchwork strips side by side (their long sides) until you have the balance of color and design that makes you happy. Then stack them up in sequence and head for the sewing machine.

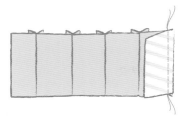

Step 6

6 With right sides together and using a ¼" seam allowance, sew the patchwork strips side by side in your chosen sequence. Press all seams open.

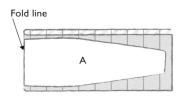

Step 7

7 Fold the patchwork in half lengthwise, and then cut the Cinch Front using pattern piece A on the fold.

8 With the wrong side of the Cinch Back against the interfacing piece, baste around all edges using a ⅛" seam allowance.

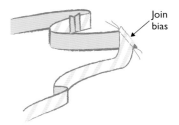

Step 9

9 With right sides together, join all the bias strips together (with 45-degree angle seams) for the edging to create one continuous piece.

10 With wrong sides together, fold the bias edging in half lengthwise and press a crease.

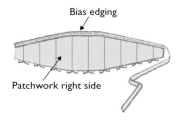

Step 11

11 With right sides together, layer the unfinished edges of the bias edging along one of the long edges of the patchwork Cinch Front, and machine-baste using a ⅛" seam allowance. Trim off the excess edging length at the end.

12 Repeat Step 11 with the excess bias edging along the other long edge of the patchwork Cinch Front.

Sew and Attach Ties

13 With right sides together, fold one of the tie pieces in half lengthwise and press. After pressing, trim one end off at a 45-degree angle.

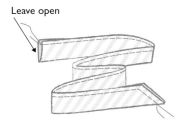

Step 14

14 With right sides together and with a ¼" seam allowance, sew the length of one of the ties along the unfinished edges and across the angled end to finish, leaving the opposite end open. Trim the seam allowance off the angled point, pull the tie through to the right side, and press well.

15 Repeat Steps 13 and 14 with the remaining tie.

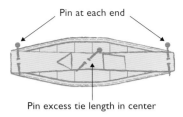

Pin at each end

Pin excess tie length in center

Step 16

Finish Cinch

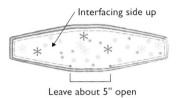

Interfacing side up

Leave about 5" open

Step 18

16 With the right side of the patchwork Cinch Front facing up, lay each of the raw-edge ends of the ties at each end of the Cinch Front and pin in place. Fold and pin the excess tie lengths in the center of the Cinch Front to keep them away from the edges.

17 Machine-tack the ends of the ties at the edges of the Cinch Front.

18 Layer the right side of the Cinch Back over the ties and Cinch Front, aligning all edges, and pin in place. Sew around all but about 5 inches of the entire Cinch perimeter using a ½" seam allowance, as shown in the figure above. Begin and end with a backstitch.

19 Trim off the seam allowance corners, and clip the curved areas. Reach inside to unpin the ties, and use them to help you pull the entire Cinch through to the right side. Smooth and poke out all edges and corners and press well, also turning in and pressing the open 5" length by ½".

20 You can choose to close the opening by blind-stitching by hand from the back side, or you could topstitch the entire perimeter of the Cinch, depending on the look you want.

–Thank You Notebook–

Thank You Notebook

*W*elcoming baby into your home usually also means welcoming a lot of gifts for you and baby from loved ones. Everyone loves a handwritten note. A written expression of gratitude is no different, and this project makes a special, portable place for you to keep all of your handwriting supplies. I have always found that the task of writing thank-you notes is something that most easily fits into my schedule in small doses over time. This often means that I'm sneaking in a few at the park, a few on a road trip, and maybe a few while waiting for dinner to be done. Tucking them into this little notebook until your next trip to the mailbox just might help you, too.

Materials

Light- to medium-weight woven fabric:

- ½ yard for Outer Cover
- ½ yard for Inner Cover and pockets
- ½ yard for bias binding and Button Loop

At least 12" × 22" of heavy-duty, double-sided fusible interfacing (very firm)

At least 9" × 12" of mid-weight, single-sided fusible interfacing (firm but fluid)

Button in the size of your choice (I used 1½" diameter)

Approximately ½ yard of ⅜"-wide cotton elastic

Finished Dimensions: 9" × 12½" × 1½" when closed

My Color Notes

I couldn't resist selecting fabrics that coordinate with my favorite collection of stationery, of course. However, I was sure to use a larger than life print for the outer sides of the notebook, a bright complement for the binding, and a quieter, smaller scale print for in the insides. Following this formula, no matter the palette, will give you something gorgeous.

Measure and Cut

1   Cut one 12" × 20" rectangle from the outer fabric for the Outer Cover.

2   Cut one 12" × 20" rectangle from the inner fabric for the Inner Cover.

3   Cut one 9" × 12" rectangle from the inner fabric for the large Slip-in Pocket.

NOTE: The following pieces for the inner pockets are sized to fit 3½" × 5" notecards and envelopes. You may choose to cut them a bit larger if you typically use larger notes. The overall notebook project dimensions will accommodate holding notes up to about 4" × 6". Notes larger than that will require that you resize the overall notebook dimensions as well.

4   Cut three 9" × 4½" rectangles from the inner fabric for the Elasticized Pockets.

5   Cut one 5" × 7" rectangle from the inner fabric for the Stamp Pocket.

6   Cut one 2" × 6" rectangle from the inner fabric for the Pen Loops.

7   Cut enough 4¼"-wide bias strips from the binding fabric to join a total length of approximately 2 yards for the edge binding.

8   Cut one 1½" × 7" rectangle from the binding fabric for the Button Loop (this length corresponds to a 1½" button).

9 Cut two 8½" × 12" rectangles from the heavy, double-sided fusible interfacing.

10 Cut one 1½" × 12" rectangle from the heavy, double-sided fusible interfacing.

11 Cut one 8" × 12" rectangle from the mid-weight, single-sided fusible interfacing.

12 Cut three 5" lengths of elastic for the elasticized pockets.

Sew the Notebook Elements

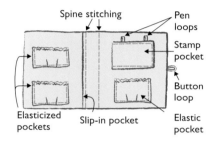

The above figure shows the overall configuration of the inside of the Thank You Notebook for reference as you move through the assembly and sewing steps.

13 Fold both long edges of the Pen Loop rectangle toward the wrong side to meet in the center, and press. Fold in half lengthwise once more to conceal the raw edges, and press again. Topstitch through all four layers down the center, and press.

14 Press all four edges of the Stamp Pocket rectangle ½" toward the wrong side.

Step 15

15 Cut the sewn Pen Loop length in half. Then fold each of those lengths in half. Place them at the wrong side of one of the long sides of the Stamp Pocket with their raw edges in line with the raw edge of the pressed fold. Pin in place about an inch or two away from each side of the center of the Stamp Pocket.

16 Topstitch the folded edges of the Stamp Pocket in place all around the perimeter of the rectangle, going over and securing the Pen Loops, ¼" away from the edge. Press well.

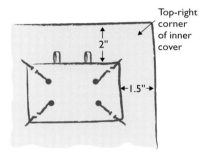

Step 17

17 Position the Stamp Pocket onto the right side of the Inner Cover in the upper-right side. The right edge of the Stamp Pocket should be roughly 1½" from the right edge of the Inner Cover, and the top edge (the Pen Loops edge) should be roughly 2" from the top edge of the Inner Cover. Pin in place.

Step 18

18 Using one of the three 9 × 4½" rectangles, make an inverted box pleat on one of the 9" edges by doing the following: fold it in half with right sides together; sew a line that is parallel to the fold, 1" away from the fold, and 1" in length. Finish with a backstitch. Open the fold, disperse the pleat on either side of the seam, and press.

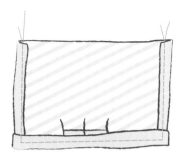

Step 19

19 Fold in both short edges and the pleated edge ½" toward the wrong side and press. Then topstitch these folds in place in a continuous U-shape ¼" from the edge. Press well.

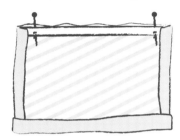

Step 20

20 Pin one of the 5" elastic lengths along the remaining unfinished edge of the Elasticized Pocket on the wrong side, with its ends right up against the raw edges of the folded-in sides. Machine-tack these two ends of the elastic in place.

21 Fold this top edge, turning the elastic within the fold, down toward the wrong side of the pocket, and zigzag-stitch the entire length while at the same time stretching the elastic to accommodate the length of the pocket. Begin and end with a backstitch.

22 Repeat Steps 18–21 with the remaining two Elasticized Pocket rectangles and two elastic lengths.

23 Position one of the elasticized Pockets below the Stamp Pocket on the right side of the Inner Cover in the lower right-hand side. The right edge of the Elasticized Pocket should be roughly 1½" from the right edge of the Inner Cover, and the bottom edge of the pocket should be roughly 1½" from the bottom edge of the Inner Cover.

Pin in place. Keep in mind that the top elasticized edge of the pocket will need to be stretched just a bit as you pin it to keep the right and left edges of the pocket at a 90-degree angle with the top and bottom edges.

24 Once you have the positioning of the Stamp Pocket and the Elasticized Pocket to your satisfaction, place one of the 8½" × 12" heavy, double-sided interfacing pieces on the wrong side of the Inner Cover, directly behind the side with the pinned-on pockets, aligning the interfacing with the right-hand corners. Press in a few places with the iron to lightly fuse the interfacing in place.

25 Stitching ⅛" from the edges, and beginning and ending with a backstitch, topstitch through all three layers (pockets, Inner Cover, and interfacing) to attach the pockets to the Inner Cover. Sew a U-shape starting from the top-left corner of the Stamp Pocket, going across the top, turning down the right side, and then finishing across the bottom, so that the opening of the pocket is at the left. For the Elasticized Pocket, sew all three sides, leaving the top elasticized side open.

26 Layer the 8" × 12" single-sided, fusible interfacing with its fusible side down onto the wrong side of the 9" × 12" Slip-in Pocket, aligning just one of their 12" edges. Press from both sides to fuse.

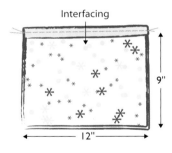

Steps 27 and 28

27 Step 26 should leave you with a 1" strip of excess down the other 12" edge of the Slip-in Pocket. Fold this edge in ½" toward the wrong side to meet the edge of the interfacing, and press a crease. Fold in ½" again to wrap the fold over the edge of the interfacing, and press another crease.

28 Machine-stitch through all layers of the folded edge and interfacing ¼" from the edge to hem the Slip-in Pocket.

29 Keeping the hemmed edge of the Slip-in Pocket at the right-hand side, position the wrong side of the two remaining elasticized pockets onto the right side of the Slip-in Pocket, with their elasticized edges oriented to the top. Pin in place.

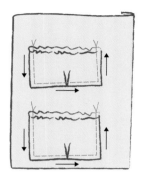

Step 30

30 Sew each of the two remaining Elasticized Pockets in place on their right-hand, bottom, and left-hand sides, keeping your stitch line ⅛" from the edge of the pockets and beginning and ending with a backstitch.

31 With the hemmed edge at the right-hand side, layer the Slip-in Pocket's wrong side onto the right side of the Inner Cover, aligning their left-hand, top, and bottom edges (be sure to refer to the layout illustration for reference). Machine-baste the Slip-in Pocket to the Inner Cover across the top, left, and bottom edges with a ¼" seam allowance.

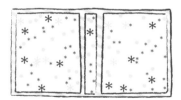

Step 32

32 Flip the Inner Cover over on the ironing board with its wrong side facing up. On top of that, place the remaining 8½" × 12" double-sided fusible rectangles on the opposite side edge from the interfacing that you placed in Step 24. Now lay the 1½" × 12" double-sided fusible rectangle between the others, centered. (This leaves two small, vertical gaps between the three pieces of interfacing.) Refer to the previous figure for correct placement.

33 Once all three interfacing pieces are neatly in place, lay the wrong side of the Outer Cover rectangle over all pieces with the right side facing up, and matching all four corners. Gently press in place with an iron to fuse the Outer Cover to the interfacings. Then carefully turn all the components over and press from the Inner Cover side as well, so that all the interfacings are sandwiched and fused between the Inner and Outer Covers.

34 Going through both inner and outer layers, machine-stitch a row of spine stitching in each of the two small, vertical gaps that are created between the three interfacing pieces.

35 Fold both long edges of the Button Loop rectangle toward the wrong side to meet in the center and press. Fold in half lengthwise once more to conceal the raw edges and press again. Topstitch through all four layers down the center and press.

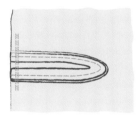

Step 36

36 Loop the Button Loop into a U-shape and align its two raw ends with the side edge of the Outer Cover's back in the center. (The Outer Cover's back is the side that has the Stamp Pocket on it.) Machine-baste the loop's ends side by side into place, using a ¼" seam allowance.

37 Join all of the 4¼"-wide bias strips with right sides together at 45-degree angles, end to end, to create one single length of bias that is about 2 yards long. Trim and press the seam allowances open.

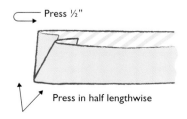

Press ½"

Press in half lengthwise

Step 38

38 Trim one end of the bias length bluntly at a 90-degree angle and press back about ½" of that end toward the wrong side. Then fold the bias binding in half lengthwise with wrong sides together, and press a crease throughout the entire length.

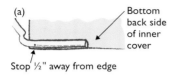

Step 39

39 With raw edges of the bias binding and the notebook aligned, and beginning about an inch from the blunt, pressed end of the bias binding, lay the bias against the Inner Cover of the notebook at the bottom of the back side. (a) Begin sewing through all layers with a ½" seam allowance until you reach ½" away from the corner edge, and then stop and backstitch. (b) Fold the binding at a right angle away from the notebook, forming an angled fold. (c) Then fold back down again the opposite way, forming a straight fold in line with the sewn edge of the notebook.

40 Repeat Step 39 (from [a]) on the other three corners of the notebook and bias binding.

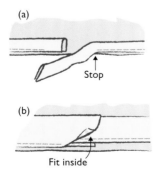

Step 41

41 Stop sewing when you are an inch or so away from the pressed end of the bias binding where you began in Step 39. Now open the creased fold of the pressed end of the binding (a) and trim the excess length off the other end of the binding so that it can rest inside the folded layers of the first (b).

42 Replace the pressed end of the bias binding to wrap around and encase the opposite end, and make a finishing line of stitching to connect to the starting and stopping points.

43 Turn the binding up over the edge of the notebook and seam allowances and press.

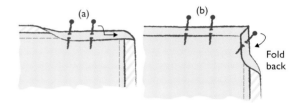

Step 44

44 At the corners of the Inner Cover, notice that the bias binding has formed a nice mitered corner. You can create this same mitered corner on the Outer Cover side, too. (a) With the Outer Cover facing you, fold down the binding to cover the stitch line and smooth this fold all the way beyond the edge of the notebook. This makes the binding form an angled fold at the corner. (b) Simply turn this angle back in toward the notebook to cover the next side's stitching, and you have formed the mitered corner. Pin in place.

45 From the Outer Cover side, topstitch the edges of the binding in place around the entire perimeter of the notebook, keeping your stitch line as consistently close to the edge of the binding as possible, and also making sure that your stitch line is going through the binding on the Inner Cover side. Press well on both sides.

46 Finish by hand-sewing the button in place at the center of the front right edge of the notebook's Outer Cover, making sure it's in line with the Button Loops wrapping forward from the back.

Flower Bed Slippers

Flower Bed Slippers

*P*regnancy and motherhood aren't always a bed of roses, but having some simple comforts can help smooth the rough spots. While it is important to sit with your feet up as much as you can during and after pregnancy, reality keeps you on your feet very often. So pamper yourself or a loved one with these sweet slippers. The shape and assembly are very basic, and the beauty is in the details. A sculptural fabric flower grows across the upper panel and sends rays of light in the form of running stitches over your toes. You can customize your slippers with as many fabric flowers as you wish or add embroidered details to your heart's desire.

Materials

Medium-weight woven cotton fabric:

- ¼ yard for Upper Panel
- ⅛ yard for Band
- ⅝ yard for Sole Lining (flannel is a great choice)
- Scraps approximately 2" × 20" for fabric flower

¼ yard Ultrasuede for Sole Bottom

¼ yard of 22"-wide heavy-duty, double-sided fusible interfacing

At least 12" × 12" of 1"-thick foam (try to find fairly dense foam)

At least 6" × 12" of cotton quilt batting

Embroidery floss and embroidery needle

Flower Bed Slippers pattern pieces inside the pocket

> **Finished Dimensions:**
> **S/M** 4¼" × 9½" × 2½" **M/L** 4¼" × 10½" × 2½"

My Color Notes

I chose to work with very naturalistic colors for the outer top of these slippers so that all of the pretty details would come in through form and texture. I did, however, add some depth of color around the outer edges, the bottom soles, and the lining in order to hide a bit of wear.

Trace and Cut

1   Trace and cut patterns **A, B,** and **C** on pattern page 2 in your desired size: On the Sole Lining and Sole Bottom (**A**), be sure to mark the center heel, center toe, and the two single notches at the inner edge. Also mark the inner edge of the Sole Cushion and Sole Interfacing (**B**) and the Upper Panel (**C**).

2   Cut two Sole Lining pieces (**A**) from the lining fabric after folding the fabric, so that you are cutting two opposite pieces at once. Mark the inner edges and center heel.

3   Cut two Sole Bottom pieces (**A**) from the Ultrasuede after folding the fabric, so that you are cutting two opposite pieces at once. Mark the inner edges, single notches, and center heel.

4   Trace the Sole Cushion (**B**) onto the foam once, then flip the pattern on to the wrong side and trace again, so that you have a right and left sole. Mark the inner edges. Using either an electric knife or a really sharp pair of scissors, cut the foam on the traced lines, making sure you aren't cutting the foam at any angle other than perpendicular to the foam surface. Take your time and cut only a little at a time to get the most accurate shape possible.

5   Trace the Sole Interfacing (**B**) onto the fusible interfacing, then flip the pattern on to the wrong side and

trace again, so that you have a right and left interfacing. Cut the interfacing pieces and mark the inner edges.

6 Cut four Upper Panels (**C**) after folding the Upper Panel fabric twice, so that you are cutting four layers at once to have two pieces that oppose the two other pieces. Mark the inner edges, basting dots, and center toe.

7 Cut two Upper Panels (**C**) from the quilt batting after folding the batting, so that you are cutting two pieces at once. Mark the inner edges.

8 Cut two Bands that each measure 1¾" wide and 26½" long for the M/L slippers or 1¾" wide and 25" long for the S/M slippers.

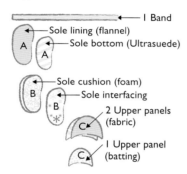

NOTE: After you've cut all the pieces, it's a good idea to divide them into right and left pieces to avoid any confusion before you begin sewing. The figure above details the pieces for each slipper.

Prepare the Upper Panel and Sole Bottom

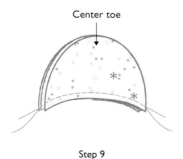

Step 9

9 First place two Upper Panel fabric pieces right sides together, and then layer the Upper Panel batting onto the wrong side of either fabric piece, making sure all the inner edges are aligned. Sew across the bottom curved edge using a ½" seam allowance. Clip the curved seam allowances, and then turn it right side out so that the batting is sandwiched between the wrong sides of the Upper Panel pieces. Press well.

10 Machine-baste through all three layers of the Upper Panel between the basting dots (don't backstitch), leaving a few inches of thread and bobbin slack on both ends.

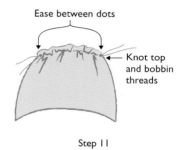

Step 11

11 Alternate tugging on the top thread at each end and gathering the material with your hands to just slightly ease up the toe of the Upper Panel to form a nice rounded toe. Avoid any gathered folds—just a smooth easing. Pull the bobbin threads to the top, and knot them together with the top threads at each end.

12 Using six strands of embroidery floss and an embroidery needle, make several rows of running stitches through all layers of the Upper Panel in a ray design from the lower-outer corner. (You can choose to make any style of embroidery in this step.) Keep all stitching about an inch away from the edges of the Upper Panel.

13 Matching the inner sides, center the fusible interfacing within the wrong side of the Sole Bottom. Hold in place as you flip it over so that you can press from the Ultrasuede side to fuse the two pieces together.

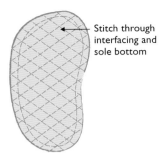

Stitch through interfacing and sole bottom

Step 14

14 Sew several rows of stitching at an angle across the Sole Bottom at an even distance from each other and through both the Ultrasuede and interfacing layers. Repeat stitching in the opposite direction to create a quilted diamond pattern. (This is really easy if you first draw your sewing lines onto the interfacing side, which you can then trace with your sewing.)

Assemble and Finish the Slippers

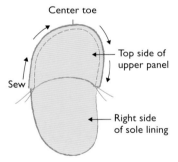

Center toe

Top side of upper panel

Sew

Right side of sole lining

Step 15

15 With the inner side of the Upper Panel against the right side of the Sole Lining, and aligning the center toe and inner edge marks, machine-baste together around the Upper Panel piece using a ⅜" seam allowance.

16 With right sides together and using a ½" seam allowance, sew the opposite ends of the Band together and press the seam allowance open.

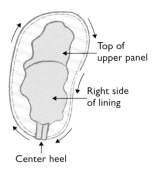

Top of upper panel

Right side of lining

Center heel

Step 17

17 With right sides together, align the seam of the Band with the center heel mark of the Sole Lining, and pin in place. Sew the Band to the perimeter of the joined Upper Panel and Sole Lining using a ½" seam allowance, carefully maintaining a consistent seam allowance around the curves. Clip the curved seam allowances.

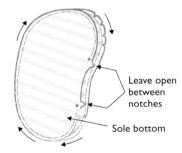

Leave open between notches

Sole bottom

Step 18

18 With right sides together, align the seam of the Band with the center heel mark of the Sole Bottom and pin in place. Beginning at one of the single notches, and using a ½" seam allowance, sew the Band to the Sole Bottom all around the perimeter, but stop at the other single notch, so that the space between the single notches on the inner edge is left open. Be sure to backstitch at the beginning and end to secure the seam. Clip all curved seam allowances.

19 Turn the slipper right side out, and finger-press all seam allowances toward the wrong side of the Band.

20 Making sure that you orient the Sole Cushion in the same direction as the slipper, slide the foam into the opening left in the Sole Bottom/Band seam. (This might require folding it a bit.) Continue to work with the foam inside the slipper until you have all the seams aligned with the top and bottom edges of the Sole Cushion, and also try to keep all seam allowances against the wrong side of the Band. Once all is in place, press the Sole Bottom from the outside to fuse the interfacing through to the Sole Cushion.

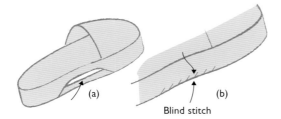

Step 21

21 (a) Wrap the inner unfinished edge of the Sole Bottom up against the foam, then fold the unfinished edge of the Band with the wrong sides together and place down over the Sole Bottom to close the open seam. (b) Blind-stitch them together. Press the seams of the slipper well all around the perimeter.

22 Machine-baste both long edges of the 2" × 20" scrap for the fabric flower.

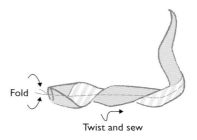

Step 23

23 Turn and fold the two end corners to overlap each other, and place them under the sewing machine foot. Lower the needle into the folded end, and then twist the length of the strip several times before sewing down the middle of the twisted length. (This step is to be done with no particular perfection, but it helps add some interest and dimension to the fabric before it's twisted into a flower shape.)

24 Begin at the folded end of the strip, and spiral the fabric into a rosette until you have about a 6" tail left at the other end. Stick a pin through the rosette to hold the layers together. Begin whipstitching the underside of the rosette together, going through a few layers of the spiral at a time, all around, until it feels secure.

25 Place the wrong side of the rosette at the outer edge of the Upper Sole and begin hand-stitching it into place from the inner side of the Upper Sole. Once the rosette is secure, you can begin to twist, turn, and hand-stitch the remaining tail of the fabric strip across the edge of the Upper Sole.

26 Repeat Steps 9–25 with all remaining pieces for the opposite slipper.

—Four Corners Blouse—

Four Corners Blouse

I can remember sitting on one of those jointed buses in San Francisco with my then 10-month-old son, Joseph. The bus was packed with people and I was sitting right at the edge of the joint so that every time we took a turn, several standing strangers practically brushed right across my face. And, of course, baby Joseph was fussing to nurse right then and there, and I wasn't wearing a shirt that exactly facilitated modesty. Joseph's pleading won out over modesty, and I remember thinking then, that I had officially nursed everywhere. This blouse, however, is designed to help you maintain comfort and some modesty, should you care about that sort of thing. So you can nurse your hungry baby to the four corners of the earth and back. Another reason this blouse is named "Four Corners" is because the entire garment is built from nothing but rectangles. The decorative buttons and loops lend beautiful, handcrafted details to the blouse, but getting down to business with baby is as simple as untying one back tie.

Materials

Lightweight cotton voile or woven fabric with similar fluid drape:

- ½ yard of contrast fabric for Yoke, Placket, Straps, Ties
- 1⅓ yards of printed fabric for Front and Back Panels, Button Loops

12 buttons, ⅝" diameter

1"-wide elastic

Finished Dimensions:
S/M Bust: 36–38", Upper Hip: 39–41", Length: 25"
M/L Bust: 39–41", Upper Hip: 41–43", Length: 26"

My Color Notes

I made Angela's blouse from a very feminine printed cotton voile. While there is lots of color, the print is small and fine so the result is sweet. I paired it with the even smaller tonal blue print, which picks up the tiniest detail of blue from the main print and buttons.

Measure and Cut

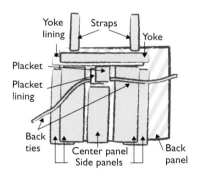

NOTE: The above diagram will help you understand the correct orientation of each piece for assembly as you cut out the rectangles.

1   Cut the following rectangles (square on the fabric's grain) from the solid fabric, being sure to follow the specific dimensions for your desired size:

- Yoke—2½" × 18½" for the S/M or 2½" × 19½" for the M/L. Cut one for the Yoke, and one for the Yoke Lining.

- Placket—3½" × 6½" for the S/M or 3½" × 7½" for the M/L. Cut one for the Placket and one for the Placket Lining.

- Straps—5½" × 18" for either size. The strap length may be adjusted to your specific measurements after you try it on. Cut two.
- Back Ties—2" × 36" for either size. Cut two.

2 Cut the following rectangles (square on the fabric's grain) from the printed fabric, being sure to follow the specific dimensions for your desired size:

- Front Side Panels—9" × 18" for the S/M or 10" × 19" for the M/L. Cut four.
- Center Panel—7" × 13" for either size. Cut one.
- Back Panel—21" × 23" for the S/M or 22" × 24" for the M/L. Cut one.
- Button Loops—1" × 36" for either size. Cut one.

3 Cut one 17" length of 1"-wide elastic for the S/M or one 18" length for the M/L.

4 Fold the Yoke in half lengthwise, and use a fabric marker to make a mark, or the iron to press a crease, at the center along one of the long edges.

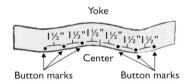

Step 5

5 From the center mark on the Yoke, measure 1½" to each side and make marks for Button Loops. From those marks, measure another 1½" away, and make two more marks. Then make a third set of marks another 1½" away from the second Button Loop marks. See the above figure to check your markings.

6 Fold the Placket in half widthwise (on one of the 3½" sides) and use a fabric marker to make a mark, or the iron to press a crease at the center.

7 Repeat Step 6 on both lengthwise sides of the Placket to mark the center of the side edges. Those center marks will serve as Button Loop marks.

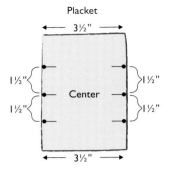

Step 8

8 Mark two more Button Loop marks on each side edge that are 1½" above the center mark and 1½" below the center mark. See the above figure to check your markings.

Baste the Center and Side Panels

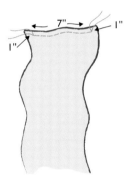

Step 9

9 Using a ½" seam allowance and beginning and ending 1" away from the edge, machine-baste one of the 7" sides of the Center Panel and leave plenty of thread slack at both ends.

10 Tug on the top thread of one end to pull up the bobbin thread, and knot them together. At the other end, pull on the top thread to draw the fabric into a gather, and reduce the width of the Center Panel until it is 3½" wide. Now knot the loose ends to secure the gathers. Press.

11 Using a ½" seam allowance and beginning and ending 1" away from the edge, machine-baste one of the shorter sides of the Side Panels and leave plenty of thread slack at both ends. Repeat with the remaining three Side Panels.

12 Tug on the top thread of one end to pull up the bobbin thread, and knot them together. At the other end, pull on the top thread to draw the fabric into a gather, and reduce the width of the Side Panels until it is 6½" wide (S/M) or 7" wide (M/L). Now knot the loose ends to secure the gathers. Press. Repeat with the remaining three Side Panels.

Sew the Blouse

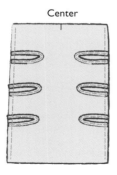

Cut twelve 3" loops

Step 13

13 With wrong sides together, fold the Button Loop strip lengthwise and press a crease down the center. Now fold the long edges of the Button Loop toward the wrong side until they meet at the center line, fold in half lengthwise again, and press. Topstitch through all folded layers so that you are left with a ¼"-wide strip. Press. Cut the 36" length into twelve 3" Button Loops.

Center

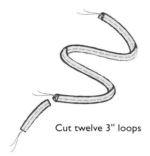

Step 14

14 Fold six of the topstitched Button Loops in half and place them on the right side of the Placket at each of

the Button Loop marks, with their raw ends in line with the side edges of the Placket. Pin them in place, and then baste along the Placket edge using a ½" seam allowance to hold the Button Loops in place.

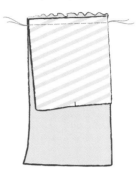

Step 15

15 With right sides together and using a ⅝" seam allowance, sew the unmarked 3½" side of the Placket to the gathered side of the Center Panel. Press the seam allowances up toward the Placket.

16 With right sides together, fold one of the Back Ties in half lengthwise and press a crease. Now sew the folded Back Tie using a ¼" seam allowance from the long raw edges, and across one of the ends. Clip the corner seam allowance at an angle. Use a safety pin or a turning tool to turn it right side out, and press. Repeat with the remaining Back Tie.

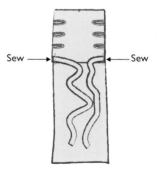

Sew →   ← Sew

Step 17

17 Align the unfinished ends of the Back Ties in the bottom corners of the Placket, just above the seam between the Placket and the Center Panel. Machine-baste both ties in place using a ½" seam allowance.

18 With right sides together and using a ⅝" seam allowance, sew one of the Side Panels to the joined Placket/Center Panel, making sure to have the gathered edge of the Side Panel aligned with the Placket top edge. Repeat with another Side Panel piece. Press all seam allowances in toward the center.

Step 19

19 With the panel pieces joined in Step 18, fold and press ¼" of their side and bottom edges toward the wrong side. Fold the three edges in once more ¼", and topstitch using a ⅛" seam allowance, to make a continuous rolled hem on the sides and bottom. Press well from both sides. Set aside.

20 Fold the remaining six topstitched Button Loops in half and place them on the right side of the Yoke at each of the button loop marks, with their raw ends in line with the edge of the Yoke. Pin them in place, and then machine-baste along the Yoke edge using a ½" seam allowance to hold the Button Loops in place.

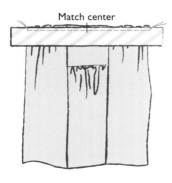

Match center

Step 21

21 With right sides together, aligning center marks, and using a ⅝" seam allowance, sew the top of the joined Placket/Side Panels/Center Panels to the bottom of the Yoke (the side with the Button Loops). Keep the pieces right sides together for now.

22 Lay the remaining two gathered Side Panel pieces out next to each other with their right sides facing up and the gathered edges oriented to the top. Mark the right edge of the left piece and the left edge of the right piece.

Step 23

23 Fold and press ¼" of the marked edges of the Side Panels toward their wrong side. Fold the edges in ¼" toward the wrong side once more and topstitch using a ⅛" seam allowance. Press well from both sides.

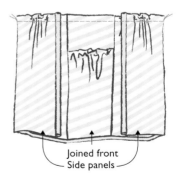

Joined front
Side panels

Step 24

24 Lay the joined pieces from Step 21 with the wrong sides of the Placket and Panels facing up. Lay the right side of the Side Panels down on top of these joined pieces so that the Side Panels' unfinished side edges are in line with the right and left side edges of the Yoke, the gathered edges of the Side Panels are in line with the sewn edge of the Yoke, and the hemmed edges of the Side Panels are facing in. See the previous figure to be sure you have all the pieces aligned correctly.

25 Sew the three layers together using a ⅝" seam allowance along the top of the Side Panels, in the same seam line as you did in Step 21. Press all seam allowances up toward the wrong side of the Yoke. From the right side, press the Yoke Button Loops against the Yoke, and the Placket Button Loops against the Placket. Press the Back Ties away from the Placket.

26 With right sides together, fold a strap piece in half lengthwise and sew only the long, unfinished edges together using a ½" seam allowance. Turn right side out and press with the seam out one of the outer edges. Repeat with the remaining strap piece.

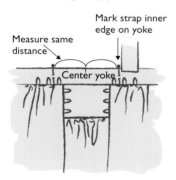

Step 27

27 To sew the Straps into the best position, you should try on the front by pinning the blouse front to your bra straps at the front and under your arms to hold it in place, making sure the Placket is centered on you. Then lay the Straps over your shoulders coming off the front, and mark with a pin on the Yoke where you want the inner edge of the Strap to be. (You may want to trim the ends of the straps at a bit of an angle so that once sewn to the front Yoke, they will lay smoothly on your shoulders.) After you've removed the blouse front, measure out the same distance from the center point

to mark the Straps' inner edge on the other side of the Yoke.

28 With right sides together, aligning one unfinished end of each Strap with the unfinished top edge of the Yoke, and with the inner edge of the Straps up against the pin mark from the previous step, machine-baste the Straps in place using a ½" seam allowance.

29 Fold the long side of the Yoke Lining in half and mark the center point with a pressed crease.

30 Fold the 3½" side of the Placket Lining in half and press a crease at the center mark. Then fold both long edges ⅝" in toward the wrong side and press a crease on both sides.

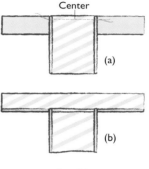

Step 31

31 With right sides together, aligning the center points and keeping the side edges of the Placket Lining folded in, sew the Placket Lining to the Yoke Lining using a ⅝" seam allowance. Press the seam allowances up toward the wrong side of the Yoke Lining, and continue the ⅝" crease along the entire edge of the Yoke Lining.

32 With right sides together, aligning center points and using a ⅝" seam allowance, sew the unfinished long edge of the Yoke Lining to the unfinished long top edge of the Yoke. This seam will sandwich the Straps between the Yoke and Yoke Lining. Press the seam allowances down against the wrong side of the Yoke.

33 Finish both side edges of the joined front pieces (including the side edges of the Yoke Lining) with a zigzag stitch or a serged edge if you have a serger. Also finish both shorter sides of the Back Panel in the same manner.

Step 34

34 With right sides together and using a ⅝" seam allowance, sew the Back Panel (the shorter edge) to the joined front pieces at each side, making sure the Yoke Lining is still opened out and included in this seam. Press the seam allowances open.

35 Fold ⅝" of the top edge of the Back Panel toward the wrong side and press, so that it is pressed along the same line as the lower edge of the Yoke Lining.

36 Fold the Yoke Lining down toward the Yoke with wrong sides together so that the seam between the Yoke and Yoke Lining is at the uppermost edge of the blouse front, and press well. Continue this fold line at the same depth all around the Back Panel piece and press a crease. This back fold will create a channel for the elastic in Step 38.

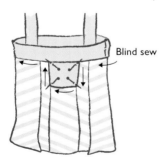

Blind sew

Step 37

37 On the wrong side of the blouse front, pin the top folded edges down at both side seams. Align all edges of the Yoke and Placket with the Yoke Lining and Placket Lining, also making sure that all of their seam allowances are hidden up and inside their wrong sides. Blind-sew or whipstitch the

linings to the seam allowances, taking care to only go through the seam allowances so that your hand stitches are not visible from the front side of the blouse. Press well from both sides.

38 Place the 1"-wide elastic (cut in the appropriate length for your size) under the top fold of the Back Panel, sandwiched between the wrong sides of the folded edge. Insert the ends of the elastic until it is just past the side seams on both sides, and pin into place.

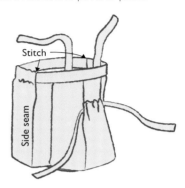

Stitch

Side seam

Step 39

39 Stitch in the ditch (right into the seams) on each of the side seams from the right side of the blouse, starting at the top edge and continuing down about an inch or so until you have secured the elastic ends in the side seam.

40 Pin the bottom fold of the elastic channel down in place, and topstitch just a scant ⅛" from the edge of the fold. (The channel will gather up a bit as the elastic is cut shorter, but just continue to stretch the elastic to accommodate a smooth seam across the Back Panel.) Press.

Step 41

41 From the inner edge of the one underneath the Side Panel, all around the Back Panel and to the inner edge of the opposite underneath Side Panel, fold and press ¼" of the bottom edge up toward the wrong side. Turn the folded edge another ¼" toward the wrong side and topstitch all around using a ⅛" seam allowance. Press.

42 Try on the blouse so that you can mark sewing placement of the Straps. (It's great to have a friend help you with this.) Once you have the Straps held where you want them, pin them in place and remove the blouse. With the Straps still pinned, you may want to invert and fold their unfinished ends toward the wrong inner sides of the Straps to conceal the raw edges before sewing in place.

43 Sew the Straps in place across the width of the Strap and on top of the elastic channel seam that you made in Step 40. You may also want to make another seam at the very top edge of the Back Panel.

44 At each Button Loop on the Yoke and the Placket, center a button over the loop and hand-sew in place. Repeat until all 12 buttons are sewn in place.

-Lingering
Layers Skirt-

Lingering Layers Skirt

As with several of the Mama projects in this book, the Lingering Layers Skirt leaves plenty of room for growing and for shrinking all within one pattern. While the graceful repetition of bias-cut curved pieces might look intimidating, they all come together quite simply. The top piece of the skirt front can first be made as a Mama panel, and then switched out later for a regular yoke-style piece that mirrors the skirt back. The pattern offers the choice of taking the front ruffle upward on a few gentle curves, leaving it straight across, or leaving if off altogether.

Materials

Light- to medium-weight woven fabric (cotton or cotton blend is ideal):

- 2 yards for skirt pieces that can be from various fabrics
- ½ yard for ruffle

⅓ yard lightweight two-way stretch lining fabric for the Mama Panel

18–20" length of ½" cotton elastic (or more if non-maternity)

Spool of perle cotton (optional for the topstitching detail)

Lingering Layers Skirt pattern pieces inside the pocket

Finished Dimensions:
Small Waist: 37/39", Hips: 43", Length: 28" **Medium** Waist: 38/40", Hips: 45", Length: 29" **Large** Waist: 40/42", Hips: 46", Length: 30"

My Color Notes

While you could combine a mix of your favorite prints, the featured solid skirt makes note of the curves by way of playful quilt-style topstitches made by hand. Within the solid skirt pieces, I let the ruffle take on a little more presence of color and texture by using sheer, iridescent linen.

Trace and Cut

1   Trace and cut the following pieces in your desired size (piece **C** stays the same for all sizes) from the Lingering Layers Skirt pattern on pattern page 3: Top Yoke (**A**), Hip Panel (**B**), Center Panel (**C**), Lower Panel (**D**), and Mama Panel (**E**). Be sure to transfer all the markings from the pattern to your traced pieces, such as notches, grain line arrows, and top edges.

2   Cut two Top Yokes (**A**) on the bias with the pattern's fold line against the fabric fold (set one aside for after baby).

3   Cut four Hip Panels (**B**) on the bias (two on the right side, two on the wrong side).

4   Cut two Center Panels (**C**) on the bias with the pattern's fold line against the fabric fold.

5   Cut two Lower Panels (**D**) on the bias with the pattern's fold line against the fabric fold.

6   Cut one Mama Panel (**E**) from the stretch lining fabric with the pattern's fold line on the fabric fold.

7   Optional: Cut two 8" × 30" (or your desired ruffle thickness by 30" length) rectangles from the ruffle fabric.

Sew the Skirt

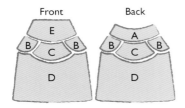

Front **Back**

The above diagram shows the piece assembly layout
for the front and back of the skirt.

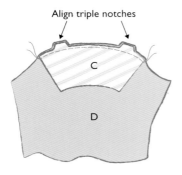

Align triple notches

Step 8

8   Take your time aligning the bottom curve of the
Center Panel with the top curve of the Lower Panel,
aligning triple notches and pinning them together. This
curve can get a little tricky and can be helped along if
you bend the top concave curve of the Lower Panel into
more of a straight line as you pin. You may also be helped
by first making a loose basting stitch along the Center
Panel bottom edge and then easing it into the top edge
of the Lower Panel.

9   Using a ⅝" seam allowance and beginning and ending
with a backstitch, sew the Center Panel and the Lower
Panel together. Clip the seams and press down toward
the Lower Panel.

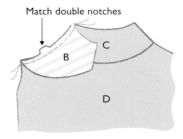

Match double notches

Step 10

10 With right sides together, matching double notches,
and using a ⅝" seam allowance, sew one of the Hip Panels
to the joined Center and Lower Panels from Step 9. Clip
the seam allowances and press down toward the Center
and Lower Panels.

11 Repeat Step 10 with an opposite Hip Panel on the
other side of the joined panels for the skirt front.

12 Repeat Steps 8–11 with the remaining Center, Lower,
and Hip Panels for the skirt back.

Steps 13 and 14

13 On both short ends of the Mama Panel, machine-
baste along the edges, starting and stopping about ½"
from the top and bottom edges and using a ½" seam
allowance and leaving some thread slack on both ends.

14 Knot together the top and bobbin threads at one
end of the basting line. Draw up the opposite end by
pulling on the top thread, and gather the side of the
Mama Panel until the short side is the same length when
compared to the side of the Top Yoke piece. Knot the
loose ends and repeat on the other side.

15 With right sides together, using a ⅝" seam allowance, and beginning and ending with a backstitch, sew the bottom edge of the Mama Panel to the top edge of the joined skirt front from Step 11 (which actually is the same as the back, so they can be used interchangeably). Take care, as you are sewing a stretch fabric to a non-stretch woven fabric; you may want to pin first and take your time sewing. Clip the curved seam and press downward.

16 With right sides together, using a ⅝" seam allowance, and beginning and ending with a backstitch, sew the bottom edge of one of the Top Yokes to the top edge of the joined skirt back. Clip the curved seam and press downward. (Reserve the remaining Top Yoke piece for refashioning the skirt after baby; see Steps 31–34.)

Hemline Variation

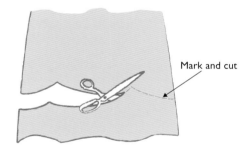

Mark and cut

Step 17

17 If you are attaching the ruffle to this skirt, and also want the front hem to take a slight scalloped curve upward on the front side, transfer the dotted line markings ("front ruffle line") with a chalk pencil from pattern piece D on the bottom edge of your front skirt panel's right side. Now cut off the skirt front bottom excess on this curved dotted line.

Step 18

18 With right sides together, using a ⅝" seam allowance and beginning and ending with a backstitch, sew the skirt front panel to the skirt back panel at each side seam. Be sure to line up the pieced intersections on each side. Press the seams open.

Step 19

19 With right sides together, using a ⅝" seam allowance, and beginning and ending with a backstitch, sew the short sides of the 8" × 30" rectangles of ruffle fabric together on both ends. Press the seams open.

20 In one pass, topstitch a line all around the perimeter of the joined ruffle ¼" from the top edge (which could be either edge), and backstitch once you've reached your starting point.

21 Similarly, topstitch several rows of stitching around the perimeter of the bottom edge that begin ¼" from the edge and then continue to be spaced about ¼" away from each other, and ending each row with a backstitch where you started it. I chose to sew four rows, which gives a nice, decorative look to the ruffle's hem.

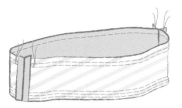

Step 22

22 Just ½" below the single topstitch line that you made in Step 20, and beginning about ½" from one of the side seams, machine-baste across and stop ½" away from the opposite side seam. Leave the beginning and ending threads loose. Repeat on the other side of the ruffle.

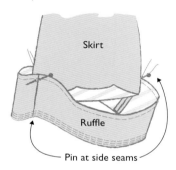

Step 23

23 At the skirt back, with the wrong side of the ruffle's top edge (the edge with only one topstitch row and one basting row) against the right side of the skirt's bottom edge, align the side seams together, and overlap the top of the ruffle by about ½" over the lower-edge of the skirt and pin at sides.

24 Knot one end of one of the basting lines from Step 22, and then begin gathering the opposite end of it by drawing up the top thread. Continue to gather and reduce the ruffle width until it fits against the bottom edge of the skirt back, and knot the loose ends of the basting lines and trim the threads. Pin the ruffle in several places to keep the basting row—about ½" above the bottom edge of the skirt.

25 Repeat Step 24 at the front side of the skirt and ruffle. The process is the same even if you are following a curved line with the front hemline, although you might be helped by finding the center point of both the ruffle and the bottom skirt edge, and lining those up as you gather and pin.

Step 26

26 Once the gathered basting line is pinned—½" above the skirt's bottom edge, topstitch the ruffle and the skirt together all around the perimeter of the skirt from the right side, stitching right into the basting line.

Finish the Waistband

27 Cut a length of the ½"-wide elastic in one of the following lengths, depending on the size you are making:

Small = 14½"

Medium = 15½"

Large = 16½"

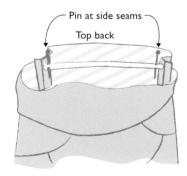

Step 28

28 On the wrong side of the skirt back, pin the elastic ends right up against each side seam and with the long edge of the elastic right against the top edge of the skirt back's top edge.

29 Beginning at one side seam, zigzag the elastic end in place with several backstitches, and then continue to zigzag the elastic to the wrong side of the skirt's top edge, stretching it out to accommodate the width of the skirt back. Finish with a zigzag backstitch at the other end of the elastic.

30 Turn the sewn elastic edge down once more ½" toward the wrong side of the skirt, and zigzag the entire perimeter this time, including the top edge of the Mama Panel; continue until you've reached the starting point and finish with a backstitch. Press well.

Alter the Skirt After Baby

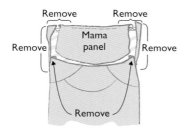

Step 31

31 Using a seam ripper, remove the stitches from the following seams, as pointed out in the previous figure:

- Top edge zigzag stitching about 2" to either side of each side seam

- Both side seams from the top to just about an inch into the Hip Panel

- Entire bottom edge of the Mama Panel

This will remove the Mama Panel from your Skirt, and the Mama Panel can now be replaced with a second Top Yoke piece.

32 With right sides together, attach the bottom edge of the new Top Yoke piece to the top edge of the joined Hip and Center Panels using a ⅝" seam allowance. Clip the curved seam allowances and press downward.

33 With right sides together, and using a ⅝" seam allowance, sew each of the side seams closed and press them open.

34 Repeat Steps 27–30 to attach elastic on the skirt's front waistband, and to finish the top edge.

-Here We Go Bag-

Here We Go Bag

*W*hile baby bags are designed to tote around all that baby needs, mom is the one who is carrying it, so it should be grown up in fashion and smart in design. This modern maxi bag is designed to take you and baby on many adventures and back again in style. Two outer-side pockets are great for quick-grab items on the go. An inner divider and more pocket options help keep all your supplies in place. When life calls for a change, there's a roll-up changing pad that slides into a corner elastic loop to keep it within reach at the top edge of the bag. Here we go!

Materials

Medium-weight or home décor-weight fabric:

- 1 yard for outer bag pieces
- 2½ yards for Panel Accent, Straps, and lining pieces
- ½ yard for the Side Panels

½ yard light- to medium-weight fabric for changing pad

At least 13" × 23" of quilt batting for changing pad

24" of ribbon for changing pad ties

3 yards of 22"-wide heavy-duty, double-sided fusible interfacing

¼ yard lightweight interfacing

22" of ½"-wide elastic

Here We Go Bag pattern pieces inside the pocket

Finished Dimensions: 13½" × 19" × 6" excluding straps

My Color Notes

I chose a very graphic and sophisticated print for this larger than life bag, but one that also echoes the modernity of the shape and design, by complementing the straight and curved lines of the bag. Choosing a smaller scale print in harmonizing hues keeps the design tame but interesting. I also added just a tiny bit of baby play by lining the pockets with a charming deer print in laminated cotton.

Trace and Cut

1   Using tracing paper, trace and cut the following pattern pieces from pattern page 4: Outer Panel and Divider (**A**), Panel Accent (**B**), Lining Panel (**G**), and Strap (**H**). Be sure to mark the interfacing lines on pattern pieces **A** and **G**.

2   Using tracing paper and a measuring device, draft and cut the following pattern pieces in the specified dimensions:

- Pocket Front (**C**)—9½" × 11" (label one of the 9½" edges as top)
- Side Panel (**D**)—7" × 14" (mark interfacing lines ¾" smaller on all sides)
- Outer and Lining Bottom Panels (**E**)—7" × 21½" (mark interfacing lines ¾" smaller on all sides)
- Lining Side Panel (**F**)—4⅛" × 14"

NOTE: When you are cutting interfacing pieces, make sure that you are following the "interfacing" lines on each pattern.

3   Cut two Outer Panels (**A**) on the fabric fold from the outer fabric.

4   Cut two Dividers (**A**) from the accent/lining/strap fabric.

5   Cut one Divider piece (**A**) on the fold from the heavy fusible interfacing.

6   Cut two Panel Accents (**B**) on the fabric fold from the accent/lining/strap fabric.

7 Cut two Pocket Fronts (**C**) from the outer fabric.

8 Cut two Side Panels (**D**) from the side panel fabric.

9 Cut two Side Panels (**D**) from the heavy fusible interfacing.

10 Cut one Outer Bottom Panel (**E**) from the outer fabric.

11 Cut one Lining Bottom Panel (**E**) from the accent/lining/strap fabric.

12 Cut one Bottom Panel (**E**) from the heavy fusible interfacing.

13 Cut four Lining Side Panels (**F**) from the accent/lining/strap fabric.

14 Cut two Lining Panels (**G**) on the fabric fold from the accent/lining/strap fabric.

15 Cut two Lining Panels (**G**) on the fold from the heavy fusible interfacing.

16 Cut four Straps (**H**), two on the right side and two on the wrong side, from the accent/lining/strap fabric (mark the outside edge).

17 Cut two Straps (**H**) from the lightweight fusible interfacing.

18 Cut bias strips from the accent/lining/strap fabric that are 1¾" wide and about 45" in length once joined.

19 Cut two pieces of ½"-wide elastic, both measuring 6½".

Construct the Outer Bag

20 With right sides together and using a ⅝" seam allowance, sew the bottom edge of the Panel Accent to the top edge of the Outer Panel. Clip the seam allowances and press toward the Outer Panel. Repeat with the remaining Panel Accent and Outer Panel.

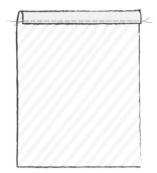

Step 21

21 Fold and press ¼" of the top edge of one of the Pocket Fronts toward the wrong side. Then fold and press another ¾" of the same edge toward the wrong side. Topstitch this fold down along the very edge of the crease to create a channel for the elastic.

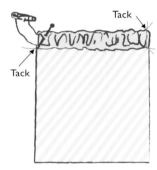

Step 22

22 Using a safety pin, feed a 6½" length of elastic through the channel until the tail end is just at the edge that you entered, and then machine-tack the elastic tail close to the edge. Continue feeding the elastic through until you've pulled the safety-pinned end out, and then use a straight pin to hold the elastic at the opposite end of the channel in place while you remove the safety pin. Machine-tack this end of the elastic at the edge of the channel.

23 With wrong sides together, fold the Pocket Front in half lengthwise and crease the center point with an iron at the other 9½" end.

24 Keep the Pocket Front folded, and then measure 1¼" from the crease and pin a mark at the edge.

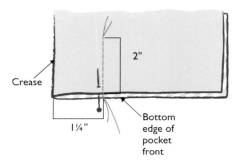

Step 25

25 Create a box pleat by sewing a 2" line of stitching at the pin mark that is perpendicular to the bottom edge, backstitching at both ends. Press the pleat evenly on each side of the stitch line.

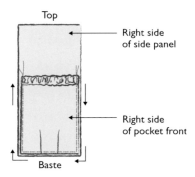

Step 26

26 Position the wrong side of the Pocket Front at the bottom edges of the right side of the Side Panel, and machine-baste together along three edges using a ½" seam allowance.

27 Repeat Steps 21–26 with the remaining Pocket Front, Side Panel, and elastic.

28 Center the Side Interfacing within the wrong side of the Side Panel and press from the right side to fuse. Repeat with the remaining Side Interfacing and Side Panel.

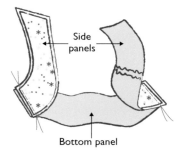

Step 29

29 With right sides together, and using a ⅝" seam allowance, join the bottom edges of each of the Side Panels to the short ends of the Bottom Panel. Press the seams open (being careful not to run your iron over the fusible interfacing).

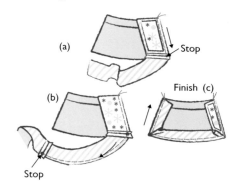

Step 30

30 Take your time and use the above three-step figure as a guide to join the Side and Bottom Panels to the Outer Panel. With right sides together and using a ⅝" seam allowance, (a) begin with a backstitch at the top edge of one of the Side Panels and the top edge of one of the Outer Panels, and sew down one side until you are ⅝" away from the bottom edge of the Outer Panel; put your needle down and take a turn (your needle should consequently go right into the seam between the Side and Bottom Panels). (b) Continue to sew along the bottom edge until you reach ⅝" away from the opposite side of the Outer Panel, and put your needle down to take a turn (again into the Side and Bottom Panel seam). (c) Finish by sewing up the final side and ending at the top edge with a backstitch.

31 Repeat Step 30 to attach the remaining Outer Panel to the Side and Bottom Panels. Trim off the corner seam allowances, clip the bottom, curved seams, and press all the seam allowances away from the Outer Panels. Turn the outer bag right side out, and press from the right side as well.

32 Fit the Bottom Interfacing into the bottom wrong side of the outer bag and smooth into all corners and edges, being sure to keep the interfacing on top of the seam allowances. Roll up a hand towel to place inside the bag to provide firm resistance so that you can press from the right side of the Bottom Panel to fuse the Bottom Interfacing into place.

Sew the Bag Lining

Step 33

33 With right sides together and using a ⅝" seam allowance, sew the top and bottom edges of the two Divider pieces together. Clip the seams, turn right side out, and press with an iron after you've smoothed the seams inside by finger pressing first.

34 Slide the Divider Interfacing in between the wrong sides of the Divider, and position neatly so that there is an even amount of excess fabric extending on either side

of the interfacing. Then fuse with an iron from both right sides of the Divider. Optionally, you can add topstitching to the top and bottom seams.

NOTE: If you'd like to add some simple pockets to the Divider, you can choose to do that now. Press ½" of all four edges of a rectangle (in your desired size) toward the wrong side, and then topstitch around the perimeter. Attach the wrong side of the rectangle to the Divider by topstitching into place on the sides and bottom of the pocket.

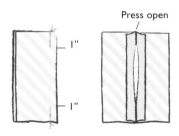

Step 35

35 With right sides together, and using a ⅝" seam allowance, sew two of the Lining Side Panels together on their long edges just for a length of 1" at the top and 1" at the bottom, leaving the center open. Repeat with the remaining two Lining Side Panels. Press the seams open.

36 With right sides together and using a ⅝" seam allowance, attach the Lining Side Panels at each short end of the Lining Bottom Panel. Press the seams open.

NOTE: If you'd like to add some simple pockets to one or both of the Lining Panels, you can choose to do that now. Press ½" of all four edges of a rectangle (in your desired size) toward the wrong side, and then topstitch around the perimeter. Attach the wrong side of the rectangle to the Lining Panel by topstitching into place on the sides and bottom of the pocket.

37 Fold the 9" elastic loop in half and tack its overlapped ends at the side of one of the Lining Panels about 4" from the top edge.

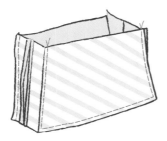

Step 38

38 In the same manner that you attached the outer Side Panels to the Outer Panels in Step 30, attach the Lining Side Panels and Lining Bottom Panel to the Lining Panel using a ⅝" seam allowance, putting the needle down to turn at the corners, and beginning and ending with a backstitch. Repeat with the remaining Lining Panel. Trim off the corner seam allowances, clip the bottom, curved seams, and press all seam allowances toward the Lining Panels. Leave the wrong side out.

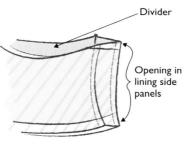

Divider

Opening in lining side panels

Step 39

39 From the right side of the lines, slide each unfinished edge of the Divider into the openings left in the two Lining Side Panels. Align their unfinished edges and sew each Lining Side Panel closed with the Divider sandwiched into the seam. Press the seams open.

40 Center each of the Panel Interfacings onto the wrong side of each of the Lining Panels (within the border of the stitch lines) and press from the right side to fuse each into place.

Assemble and Finish the Bag

41 Place the Lining inside of the Outer bag with the wrong sides together, smoothing all corners and edges into place, and aligning the top edges and the four side seams with each other. Once the Lining and Outer bag fit together well, press from all sides to fuse the interfacings. When pressing from the outside, it might be helpful to again use a rolled-up hand towel on the inside to provide some resistance.

42 Lay the right sides of two opposite Straps together before laying one of the Strap Interfacings onto the wrong side on top. Sew the two long sides of the straps and interfacing together using a ⅝" seam allowance. Clip the seams, turn them right side out, press, and topstitch ⅛" from the edges. Repeat with the remaining Strap and Strap Interfacing pieces.

43 With right sides together, join the lengths of bias strips using 45-degree seams, and trimming and pressing excess seam allowances until you have at least 45" of continuous bias length. Trim one end at a 90-degree angle and press it ½" toward the wrong side.

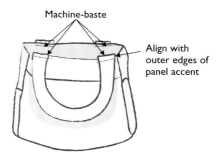

Machine-baste

Align with outer edges of panel accent

Step 44

44 Making sure you have the outer edges of the straps aligned with the outer edges of the Panel Accent pieces, pin the raw ends of the straps in line with the top edges of the outer bag on both sides. Machine-baste the straps in place using a ¼" seam allowance.

Machine-baste

Step 45

45 With right sides together and beginning with the pressed end of the bias length, lay the edge of the bias along the upper edge of the outer bag and pin all the way around until you've overlapped the pressed end by about an inch, and trim off the excess. Sew the bias to the bag's upper edge around the entire bag perimeter using a ½" seam allowance.

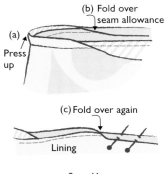

(a) Press up

(b) Fold over seam allowance

(c) Fold over again

Lining

Step 46

46 (a) Fold and press the wrong side of the bias up against the seam allowances, (b) then wrap the bias top edge around the seam allowance and (c) fold them all down toward the bag lining. By doing this, the seam you created in Step 43 should be at the very top edge of the bag, the raw edges should be concealed by the bias, and all of the bias should face into the lining.

47 Once you have the bias folded down, pressed, and pinned in place, you can either blind-sew it to the lining or topstitch on the machine using a ⅜" seam allowance. (Though hand sewing takes longer, I prefer to do that

here, because it can be a little tough getting a smooth machine stitch around the bag if you've used a really stiff interfacing.)

Cut and Sew the Changing Pad

48 Cut two 13" × 23" rectangles from the changing pad fabric, and one from the quilt batting.

49 Fold the length of ribbon in half and pin the fold in place in the center of one of the 13" edges of one of the changing pad pieces on the right side with the excess of the ribbon laying with the triangle. Machine-tack the ribbon to the edge.

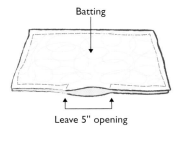

Batting

Leave 5" opening

Step 50

50 Lay the right sides of the two changing pad pieces together, and then lay the quilt batting on top of one of the wrong sides, sew around the perimeter using a ½" seam allowance, stopping about 5" away from where you started, and leaving an opening in the seam at one of the 23" sides. Clip the corners and turn the changing pad right side out.

51 Press well from the right sides, being sure to fold in the seam opening to the inner wrong side by ½". Topstitch around the perimeter using a ¼" seam allowance, thereby closing the opening in the seam.

52 You can continue to topstitch through all three layers of the changing pad to quilt it in a pattern of your choosing. I simply made some concentric rectangles about an inch apart from each other.

—Mariposa Dress and Tunic—

Mariposa Dress and Tunic

The transformation that you and your body will experience during and after pregnancy is nothing short of a gorgeous wonder. Ignore any thought that has you feeling otherwise. This pattern is designed to transform with you and your wardrobe both before and after baby arrives. The same modesty panel that accommodates your growing bosom during pregnancy will also help you maintain some privacy while nursing later. A simple change in the skirt panel's shape and cut will give you the option to make it maternity or just an empire style that you can continue to wear while nursing—and even after. Knot the wrap-around ties in back or bow them in front, on top of that cute belly. Sleeve it or go sleeveless. Adapt the length for a tunic or a dress. Spread your wings, Mama!

Materials

Light- to medium-weight woven fabric (cotton or cotton blend is ideal)

- 3 yards for dress
- 2¾ yards for tunic

½ yard lightweight woven cotton for linings and facings (cotton voile is ideal)

4" of ½"-wide cotton elastic

Mariposa Dress/Tunic pattern pieces inside the pocket

Finished Dimensions:
S/M Bust: 38/40", Waist: 44½", Hips: 44½", Length: 34" dress or 24" tunic **M/L** Bust: 40/42", Waist: 46½", Hips: 46½", Length: 36" dress or 26" tunic

My Color Notes

While I chose a graphic print for my dress, both the fact that it is a tonal, blue on blue print, and one with a linear direction, make it a flattering choice for a blossoming silhouette. Print placement has everything to do with the success of this dress design, so buying extra yardage if necessary. The color is also pretty multi-seasonal, so a lightweight cardigan and boots help me wear this dress through cooler weather.

Trace and Cut

1   Trace and cut the following pieces on pattern page 1 in your desired size: Front Bodice and Lining (**A**); Back Bodice (**B**), Back Neck Facing (**b**), which is just a smaller pattern within the Back Bodice pattern; Modesty Panel (**C**); Wrap Ties (**D**) and (**D continued**) joined together with tape; Sleeve (**E**).

2a   For the maternity version, use tracing paper and a measuring device to create the pattern for the Front Skirt Panel and Back Skirt Panel by following the specific directions below, based on the size pattern you are making and whether you are making a dress or tunic:

—OR—

2b   For the empire (non-maternity) version, use the size guide below, but skip making a Front Panel pattern and only make a Back Panel pattern, which you will use for both the front and back pieces:

- Small/Medium Dress: Front Panel 12" × 24" rectangle, Back Panel 11½" × 23" rectangle
- Small/Medium Tunic: Front Panel 12" × 14" rectangle, Back Panel 11½" × 13" rectangle
- Medium/Large Dress: Front Panel 13" × 26" rectangle, Back Panel 12½" × 25" rectangle
- Medium/Large Tunic: Front Panel 13" × 16" rectangle, Back Panel 12½" × 15" rectangle

NOTE: Once you have drawn and cut the Front and Back Panels patterns, you will need to amend the rectangles slightly to create the right shape at the top and bottom edges. As long as you are making the maternity version, you will need to do Steps 3 and 4 no matter the size, or whether you are making the dress length or the tunic length. If you are making the empire version (non-maternity) of this pattern, skip to Step 7.

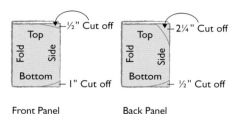

Front Panel   Back Panel

In the above figure of the Front Panel and Back Panel, notice that the two opposing longer edges are the side edge and center fold edge. Mark them accordingly so that you can keep track. Then mark the shorter edges as either top or bottom.

3 On the Front Panel, at the corner where the top edge and the side edge meet, make a mark on the side edge ½" down from the top edge.

4 From the ½" mark that you made in Step 3, draw a gently curving line from the side edge up to the top edge as shown in the figure above. Your curved line should meet the top edge about halfway across the top edge length. Trim off the excess along that curved line.

5 On the Front Panel, at the corner where the bottom edge and the side edge meet, make a mark on the side edge 1" away from the bottom edge.

6 From the 1" mark that you made in Step 5, draw a gently curving line from the side edge down toward the bottom edge as shown in the figure above. Your curved line should meet the bottom edge about two-thirds of the way across the bottom edge length. Trim off the excess along that curved edge.

7 On the Back Panel, at the corner where the top edge and the side edge meet, mark the top edge 2¼" away from the side edge.

8 From the 2¼" mark that you made in Step 7, draw a smooth curved line down along the side edge to form the hip curve and eventually meet the pattern's side edge at about halfway down, as shown in the previous figure. Trim off the excess along this curved line.

9 On the Back Panel corner where the side edge and the bottom edge meet, make a mark on the side edge ½" from the bottom edge.

10 From the ½" mark that you made in Step 9, draw a gently curving line from the side edge down toward the bottom edge as shown in the previous figure. Your curved edge should meet the bottom edge line about halfway across the pattern's bottom edge. Trim off the pattern excess from that curved edge.

11 Cut two Front Bodices (**A**), opposite, from the main fabric, and cut two Front Bodices, opposite, from the lining fabric, keeping the pattern's grain-line arrows in line with the grain of the fabric.

12 Cut one Back Bodice (**B**) after placing the pattern's center fold edge on the fabric fold.

13 Cut one Back Neck Facing (**b**) after placing the pattern's center fold edge on the fabric fold.

14 Cut one Modesty Panel (**C**) from the main fabric, and cut one from the lining fabric.

15 Cut one Front Skirt Panel from the main fabric after placing the pattern's center fold edge on the fabric fold. (Skip this step if you're making the empire version.)

16 Cut one Back Skirt Panel from the main fabric after placing the pattern's center fold edge on the fabric fold. (Cut two if making the empire version, and these will act as your front and back pieces.)

17 Cut four Wrap Ties (**D**), two on the right side and two on the wrong side, from the main fabric.

18 Cut two Sleeves (**E**), opposite, from the main fabric. (Skip this step if you're making the sleeveless version.)

19 If you are making the sleeveless version, cut two bias strips measuring 1½" wide by about 20" long from either your main fabric or your lining fabric. Set aside.

Sew the Dress/Tunic

20 After transferring the shoulder box pleat marks from the Front Bodice pattern to the Front Bodice piece, fold the fabric right side against itself to pin the two pleats in place. Repeat on both Front Bodice pieces.

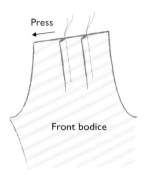

Step 21

21 Make two box pleats on the shoulder edge of the Front Bodice at a seam depth and distance as shown in the pattern markings. Begin and end with a backstitch. Press the pleat seam allowances toward the armhole. Repeat on both Front Bodice pieces.

22 After transferring the bust box pleat marks from the Front Bodice pattern to the Front Bodice piece, fold the fabric right side against itself to pin the pleats in place. Repeat on both Front Bodice pieces.

23 Make two box pleats at the under-bust edge of the Front Bodice at a seam depth and distance as shown in the pattern markings. Begin and end with a backstitch. Press the pleat seam allowances toward the side seam. Repeat on both Front Bodice pieces.

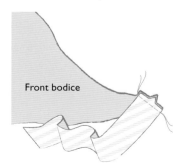

Step 24

24 With right sides together, matching single notches and using a ½" seam allowance, sew one of the Wrap Ties to one of the Front Bodice pieces, and press the seam open. Repeat with the remaining Front Bodice piece and another Wrap Tie.

25 With right sides together, and using a ½" seam allowance, sew the Modesty Panel piece to the Modesty Panel lining piece at each side and around the neck seam. Leave the shoulders and bottom open. Clip all the curved seams, turn through to the right side, and press well.

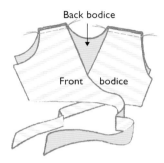

Step 26

26 With right sides together, layer both Front Bodices (making sure that the Wrap Ties are at the center) onto the Back Bodice at the shoulders. Sew across each shoulder using a ⅝" seam allowance, and press the seam allowances open.

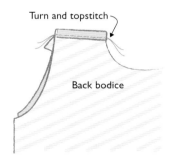

Step 27

27 Fold the Back Bodice seam allowance toward the wrong side on both shoulders, so that the raw edge meets the stitch line from Step 26, and topstitch across as shown in the figure above. Press down again.

28 Repeat Steps 20–24 on both Front Bodice Lining pieces.

29 Turn ⅜" of the Back Neck facing's outer (longer) edge toward the wrong side and topstitch a finished edge using a ¼" seam allowance. Press.

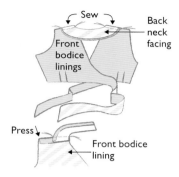

Step 30

30 With right sides together, join the Back Neck Facing with the Front Bodice Linings at the shoulder seams, using a ⅝" seam allowance. Press the seam allowances toward the Front Bodice Lining. (Though this seam does not go across the whole shoulder of the Front Bodice Lining, go ahead and press a crease across all the way at the ⅝" line.)

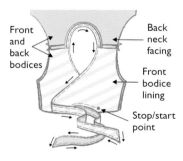

Step 31

31 Notice the stop/start points on the under-bust line of the Front Bodice pattern. Starting and ending at these points, with right sides together, and using a ½" seam allowance, sew the joined Front and Back Bodices together with the joined Back Neck Facing and Front Bodice lining, all along the top and bottom of the Wrap Ties and the neckline.

32 Trim and clip the pointed ends off the Wrap Ties, and clip the seam allowances all along the curved edges. Pull the Wrap Ties through to the right side, turn them all right side out, and press well along all stitched edges.

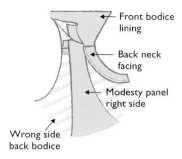

Step 33

33 Lay the lining side of the Modesty Panel against the wrong side of the Back Bodice. Line up the unfinished top shoulder edges of the Modesty Panel with the pressed, unfinished edges of the Front Bodice seam allowances, also positioning the inner edge of the Modesty Panel shoulder right up against the outer finished edge of the Back neck facing. Now layer the creased shoulder of the Front Bodice lining on top, lining up the creased shoulder edge with the shoulder seam. Pin all in place.

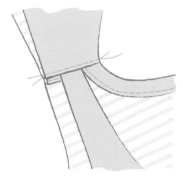

Step 34

34 Topstitch the Front Bodice lining across the whole shoulder seam as close to the creased edge as you can, backstitching at the beginning and end. (You may choose to first transfer your pins to the right side and perform this stitch line on the right side of the Front Bodice, since this will show from the outside. If so, you'll stitch just to the front side of the shoulder seam.)

35 Repeat Steps 33 and 34 at the other shoulder. Flip the Modesty Panel toward the wrong side of the front side and press at the shoulders.

36 Optional: You may choose to topstitch the Back Neck facing to the Back Bodice. If so, just press down well first, and then topstitch ⅝" away from the inner neckline edge, starting at one shoulder seam and finishing at the other—backstitching at the beginning and end.

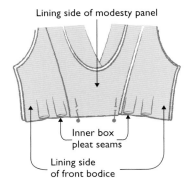

Lining side of modesty panel

Inner box
pleat seams

Lining side
of front bodice

Step 37

37 At the bottom edge of the Front Bodices, position the Modesty Panel to overlap each of the Front Bodice pieces, so that its outer edges just meet with the innermost box pleat seams on each Front Bodice piece. The bottom unfinished edges should be aligned. Pin in place at each side.

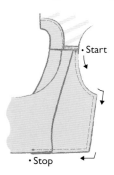

• Start

• Stop

Step 38

38 With wrong sides together, making sure all edges of the Front Bodice and the Front Bodice lining are matched up, and starting at the shoulder seam, machine-baste the outer edges of the two layers together ½" from the unfinished edges. Continue around the armhole, down the side, and across the bottom edge until you reach the innermost edge of the Front Bodice piece. (This is where the curve for the Wrap Ties begins.) This step should

catch the overlap with the Modesty Panel, and merge the Front Bodice and its lining together so that they can all be treated as one front piece for the rest of the steps. Repeat on the other side of the front.

39 With right sides together, and using a ⅝" seam allowance, sew the bottom edge of the Back bodice to the top edge of the Back Skirt panel. Also make a zigzag stitch all along the edge of this seam allowance.

40 Fold this seam line in half to find the center point of the back, and mark it with a pin on the seam allowance edge. From that center pin, measure 3" to each side, and mark those points with two more pins. You can then remove the center pin, and you should be left with two pins that are 6" apart.

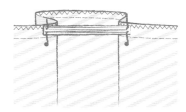

Step 41

41 Cut a piece of ½"-wide cotton elastic in a 3½" length. Use the same two pins from the previous step to pin this length of elastic at each end of the 6" distance on the seam allowance.

42 Making sure the edge of the elastic is right up against the seam line from Step 38, hold the pinned points of the edge, stretching the elastic out to the full 6" distance, and zigzag the elastic to the seam allowance, backstitching at the beginning and end. Press the seam allowances down toward the skirt.

NOTE: Follow Steps 43–46 only if you are making the maternity version of this pattern. Skip to Step 47 if you are making the empire version.

43 Fold the top edge of the Front Skirt Panel in half to find the center point, and mark it with a pin. From that center pin, measure 5" to either side and mark those points with two more pins. You can then remove the center pin. You should be left with two pins that are 10" apart.

44 Make two rows of parallel machine-basting stitches between the two pins that are $\frac{1}{4}$" and $\frac{1}{2}$" away from the top edge of the Front Skirt Panel. Be sure to leave at least 6" of thread slack at both ends of both basting lines, and do not backstitch.

45 At one end of the basting lines, tug both top threads to pull up the bobbin threads from the underside through to the top. Tie all four threads together in one knot.

Step 46

46 With right sides together, begin pinning the bottom edge of the Front Bodice to the top edge of the Front Skirt Panel from the side edges going in (let the Wrap Ties fall in and out of your way). Once you've reached the basting rows on each side, stop pinning and begin pulling on the two top threads of the loose, untied end of the basting rows to gather the skirt panel so that it fits to the Front Bodice. Once it's gathered the appropriate amount, knot the loose threads, and finish pinning to the Front Bodice.

47 With right sides together and using a $\frac{5}{8}$" seam allowance, sew the bottom edge of the Front Bodice to the top edge of the Front Skirt Panel, beginning and ending with a backstitch. You may choose to zigzag this seam allowance edge. Press all seam allowances down toward the skirt panel.

NOTE: If you are making the pattern with sleeves, follow Steps 48–53. If you are making the pattern sleeveless, follow Steps 54–58. For either version, continue again at Step 59.

48 Machine-baste the top shoulder edge of the sleeve between the pattern's basting points $\frac{1}{2}$" from the edge of the sleeve. Repeat on the remaining sleeve.

Ease sleeve

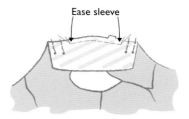

Step 49

49 With right sides together, and matching double notches, begin pinning the sleeve to the joined Front and Back Bodices at the armhole. Pin from the back edge in and from the front edge in until you meet the basting line at each end. Tie the top and bobbin threads of one end of the basting line in a knot, and begin gathering the sleeve just ever so slightly from the other end by tugging on the top thread a bit. This step helps you "ease" the sleeve onto the armhole shape, more than it actually gathers, so spread the fullness you are creating evenly, and finish pinning the sleeve to the armhole.

50 With right sides together and using a $\frac{5}{8}$" seam allowance, sew the sleeve to the armhole of the Front and Back Bodice. Clip the seam allowances and press toward the bodices.

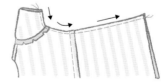

Step 51

51 With right sides together and using a $\frac{5}{8}$" seam allowance, sew the front to the back, starting at the bottom edge of the sleeve and ending at the bottom edge of the skirt panels. Be sure to line up the front and back of the armhole seam, and the front and back of the waist-line seams. Begin and end with a backstitch. Press open (and finish each edge of the seam allowances with a zigzag stitch if you wish).

52 Press $\frac{1}{4}$" of the bottom edge of the sleeve toward the wrong side, then fold in $\frac{1}{4}$" again and topstitch to make the sleeve hem. Press well.

53 Repeat Steps 48–52 on the opposite sleeve and side seam. (Continue at Step 59.)

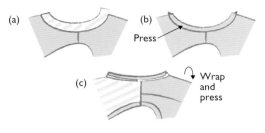

Step 54

54 Using the bias strips cut in Step 19, leave a small overhang of bias at one end, with right sides together and using a ⅝" seam allowance, sew the bias strip to the armhole edge from the front side edge to the back side edge. Clip the seam allowance. Press the right side of the bias toward the seam allowance. Then wrap the outer unfinished edge of the bias around the edge of the seam allowances and press again.

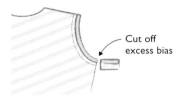

Step 55

55 Fold so that the right sides of the Front and Back are together and so that the side edges are lined up at the armhole. Trim off the excess bias from both the front and back of the armhole to be in a continuous line with the side edges.

56 With right sides together and using a ⅝" seam allowance, sew the side seam starting at the folded-over bias edge of the armhole and continuing to the bottom edge of the skirt panels. Be sure to line up the Front and Back at the waist-line seams. Begin and end with a backstitch. Press open (and finish each edge of the seam allowances with a zigzag stitch if you wish).

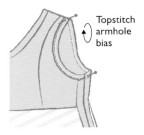

Step 57

57 Turn the bias-wrapped seam allowance again toward the inside of the armhole, so that the bias seam is at the outermost edge of the armhole and none of the bias is visible from the right side of the garment. Pin at the side seam and at the shoulder seam, and press all edges. Topstitch all around the armhole perimeter, keeping your stitch line right beside the inner fold of the bias edging and consistently even from the outer edge. Press well.

58 Repeat Steps 53–57 on the other side.

59 Turn ⅛" of the bottom skirt edge up toward the wrong side and press. Turn up ⅛" once more and topstitch all around the bottom of the skirt, passing your stitch line through the center of the folded hem. Press well.

CHAPTER

3

Baby Sewing

-Cute-as-a-Button Booties-

Cute-as-a-Button Booties

*Y*ou can hardly sew for baby without including some cuteness for the little feet. While I know you would rather spend the day kissing those tiny toes, when baby's feet need to stay warm, booties are the cutest way possible, of course. After the experiences of so many babies and so many pairs of booties, this shape and design was inspired by the need to both get the booties on and keep them on. Keeping them soft and cozy and using some of my favorite vintage buttons was also high on the list of features. Try using a flannel for the lining and your baby will thank you (one way or another). And once baby is treading a few steps, you may want to make a pair with a no-slip material on the bottom sole.

Materials

Light- to medium-weight cotton fabric:
- ¼ yard for outer pieces
- ¼ yard for lining pieces

18" × 18" cotton quilt batting

8" × 8" double-sided fusible interfacing

12" length of ½"-wide cotton elastic (I use cotton for the natural color)

2 buttons (I used 1" diameter)

Cute-as-a-Button Booties pattern pieces inside the pocket

Finished Dimensions (heel to toe):
0–3 mos 4½" **3–6 mos** 4¾" **6–9 mos** 5" **9–12 mos** 5½"

My Color Notes

What sweet feet a baby girl will have with this precious pink and yellow confection. Inspired by my collection of vintage buttons, I simply held buttons up to some of my favorite prints and decided the fabrics that way. Though the booties are cut from just one print, I placed the tongue pieces on a mostly yellow ground before cutting so that it complemented the magentas and reds of the outer pieces a bit.

Trace and Cut

1   Trace and cut patterns **B** (Sole), **B** (Toe Panel), **C**, and **D** on pattern page 2 in your desired size. Notice on the Sole and Inner Sole pattern pieces that one side is marked "inner" and one side is marked "outer." Cutting each of these patterns opposite (or one right side and one wrong side) from your materials will give you left and right booties. You may choose to mark the inner sides on all pieces to keep track as you cut and assemble.

2   Cut two Soles (**B**), opposite, from the outer fabric. Cut two, opposite, from the lining fabric. Pair the corresponding outer and lining pieces together and set them aside.

3   Cut two Toe Panels (**B**) from the outer fabric, cut two from the lining fabric, and cut two from the quilt batting.

4   Cut two Heel Panels (**C**) from the outer fabric, cut two from the lining fabric, and cut two from the quilt batting.

5   Cut two Inner Soles (**D**), opposite, from the fusible interfacing, and cut two, opposite, from the quilt batting.

6   Cut the elastic into two 3½" lengths and two 2¼" lengths.

Prepare the Toe and Heel Panels

7 Place the Toe Panel and Toe Panel lining right sides together. Then place the Toe Panel batting piece against the wrong side of the lining piece and pin through all three layers.

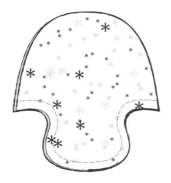

Step 8

8 Using a ¼" seam allowance, sew through all three layers from one side to the other, between dots, curving along the tongue of the Toe Panel carefully and evenly from the edge. Begin and end with a backstitch.

9 Clip the seam allowance in several places along the curves, turn the right side out, smooth the seam, and press well.

Step 10

10 Machine-baste all three layers together using a ⅛" seam allowance along the curved toe edge of the piece.

11 Repeat Steps 7–10 on the remaining Toe Panel pieces.

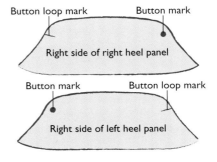

Step 12

12 Lay the outer Heel Panel pieces out with right sides facing up, and transfer the button and button loop marks onto the pieces. However, make the markings so that the positions of the marks on the right sides of the panels mirror one another, as shown in the illustration.

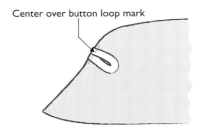

Step 13

13 Fold the 3½" length of elastic in half, overlapping the widths just slightly; then place it on the right side of the Heel Panel, centered over the button loop mark, and pin it in place once you have the two ends of elastic flush with the edges of the Heel Panel. Sew it in place using a few back-and-forth stitches at the machine, at a ⅛" seam allowance.

14 Place the outer Heel Panel and Heel Panel lining right sides together. Then place the Heel Panel batting against the wrong side of the lining, and pin through all three layers.

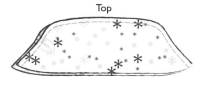

Top

Step 15

15 In one continuous seam and using a ¼" seam allowance, sew from one pointed side to the other along the top edge of the heel pieces. Begin and end with a backstitch.

16 Clip the seam allowance well, turn it to the right side, smooth the seam, and press well.

17 Machine-baste all three layers together using a ⅛" seam allowance along the bottom edge of the heel piece.

18 Repeat Steps 13–17 with the remaining heel pieces.

19 Transfer the two elastic position marks from the Heel Panel pattern to the right side of both of the Heel Panel linings.

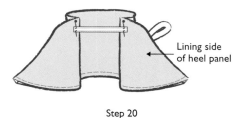

Lining side of heel panel

Step 20

20 Pin each end of the 2¼" elastic on the lining side of the Heel Panel at these two marks.

Step 21

21 Zigzag-stitch the elastic through all three layers of the Heel Panel in a straight line from one pin to the other, backstitching at the beginning and end, and stretching the elastic enough to keep the Heel Panel flat.

22 Repeat Steps 20 and 21 with the remaining Heel Panel and elastic.

Assemble the Booties

NOTE: Pair up the two Heel Panels with the two outer Sole pieces so that with right sides together, the elastic sides of the Heel Panels are facing out at you.

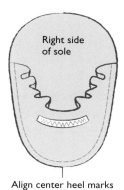

Right side of sole

Align center heel marks

Step 23

23 With right sides together, and matching up the center heel marks, pin the Heel Panel to its corresponding Sole piece. Sew them together using a ¼" seam allowance, backstitching at the beginning and end, and taking your time to keep the curved seam smooth and even from the edges.

24 Matching single notches, place the right, outer side of the Toe Panel against the right side of the Sole that was joined to the Heel in Step 23. The Toe Panel should overlap the ends of the Heel Panel on both sides. Pin in place.

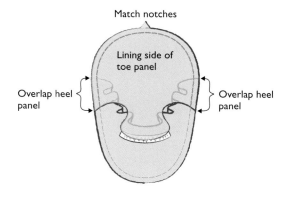

Match notches

Lining side of toe panel

Overlap heel panel

Overlap heel panel

Step 25

25 Sew the Toe Panel to the Sole around the entire curve of the toe, using a ¼" seam allowance and backstitching at the beginning and end.

26 Wedge-clip around the whole perimeter, turn the right side out, smooth the seams, and press.

27 Repeat Steps 23–26 with the remaining Heel Panel, Toe Panel, and Sole.

28 Lay the Inner Sole interfacing pieces out opposite to be sure you have a right Sole and left Sole facing up. Then fit the corresponding batting pieces on top, and give a quick press with steam from the batting side to fuse the batting to the interfacing.

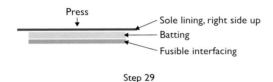

Step 29

29 Center the wrong sides of the Sole lining pieces on top of the batting sides of the Inner Soles, and press in place to fuse through all three layers.

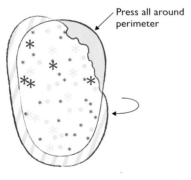

Step 30

30 Turn the Inner Sole over to the underside and use the tip of the iron to help you fold over and press the edges of the Sole lining against the underside of the Inner Sole. Continue to fuse around all edges and repeat on the other Inner Sole. (You can first run a quick hand-basting stitch all around the outermost edges of the Sole lining piece, and then drawstring them in and knot to help tighten the edges up against the underside of the Inner Sole.)

31 You can now insert the fused Inner Soles with the underside facing down into the corresponding bootie. Work with the Inner Sole until you have it situated on top of the bootie's seam allowances, and place it neatly within the perimeter seam of the Sole. Once you're satisfied with the placement, press the outer underside of the Sole to fuse the Inner Sole in place (and don't burn your fingers!). Repeat with the other bootie.

32 Using the button marks that you made in Step 12, hand-sew the button in place on each bootie, and knot to finish.

Quick Change Trousers

Quick Change Trousers

*T*hese simple and sweet baby pants double the cuteness by being reversible. The same pattern is equally adorable for a boy or a girl, and it's a welcome opportunity to mix around some of your favorite fabric prints. Folding up the cuffs will allow you to play with peeks of color from the reverse side and also leaves some growing room for those little legs. A back yoke is another fun spot to play with a little more print or splash of color. Making a few pairs of these two-in-one pants will multiply baby's wardrobe options in no time at all.

Materials

Lightweight cotton fabric:

Sizes 0–3, 3–6, 6–12 mos:

- ⅝ yard for outer side of pants
- ⅝ yard for the reverse side

Sizes 12–18 and 18–24 mos:

- ¾ yard for outer side of pants
- ¾ yard for the reverse side

½"-wide cotton elastic in one of the following lengths:

- 0–3 mos: 16" length
- 3–6 mos: 18" length
- 6–9 mos: 19" length
- 9–12 mos: 19½" length
- 12–18 mos: 20" length
- 18–24 mos: 20" length

Quick Change Trousers pattern pieces inside the pocket

Finished Dimensions:

0–3 mos Waist: 18", Unfolded length: 13" **3–6 mos** Waist: 20", Unfolded length: 15" **6–9 mos** Waist: 21", Unfolded length: 16" **9–12 mos** Waist: 21½", Unfolded length: 17" **12–18 mos** Waist: 22", Unfolded length: 18¾" **18–24 mos** Waist: 22", Unfolded length: 19½"

My Color Notes

Little Marios hardly needs any help in the cuteness department, but why not send it over the top with his multi-colored trousers? I essentially chose a primary color scheme of red, blue, and yellow, and kept the scale pretty close to the same size between the three fabrics. Each print is pretty tame and geometric, but the combination is just silly enough to be perfectly suited for a curious boy.

Trace and Cut

1   Trace and cut the following pattern pieces from pattern sheet 7 in your desired size: Front Leg (**A**)—for sizes 6–9 and up, complete full pattern **A** by tracing together w/ **A continued,** Back Yoke (**B**), and Back Leg (**C**). Be sure to mark the all notches and center mark on **B.**

2   Fold the outer fabric right sides together, and cut the Front Leg pattern once so that you end up with two opposite Front Legs.

3   Repeat Step 2 to cut the Back Yoke and Back Leg pieces.

4   Repeat Steps 2 and 3 with the reverse fabric.

Sew the Back Legs

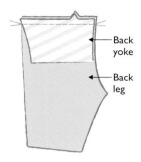

Step 5

5 With right sides together, using a ⅝" seam allowance and matching single notches and center sides, sew the right Back Yoke to the right Back Leg. Press the seam allowances down toward the wrong side of the Back Leg.

6 Repeat Step 5 with the left Back Yoke and left Back Leg.

Step 7

7 With right sides together and using a ⅝" seam allowance, sew the right and left joined Back Legs together at the curved center seam. Clip the curved seam allowance and press it open.

Step 8

8 On the fabric's right side of the joined Back Legs, topstitch the yoke seam from one side to the other just about ¼" below the seam so that you are also going through all the seam allowances. Press.

Sew the Front and Back Legs

9 With right sides together and using a ⅝" seam allowance, sew the right and left Front Legs together at the center curved seam. Clip the curved seam allowance and press it open.

Step 10

10 With right sides together and using a ⅝" seam allowance, sew the joined front to the joined back at both outer side seams. Press both seam allowances open.

11 Keeping fabric right sides together, pin the front center seam to the back center seam.

(a)

Center seam

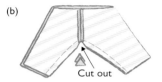

(b)

Cut out

Step 12

12 (a) Using a ⅝" seam allowance, sew from the center seam to the ankle on one side. Then begin at the center seam again and sew in the other direction to finish at the other ankle. (b) Clip the inseam seam allowance toward the center seam on each side, and then snip off a triangle of seam allowance in the center. Press the seam allowances open.

13 Fold ½" of each ankle cuff toward the wrong side and press a crease. Turn the trousers right side out.

14 Repeat Steps 5–13 with the reverse side pieces, but leave them wrong side facing out when you're finished.

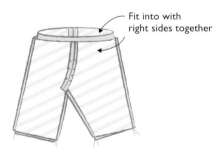

Fit into with right sides together

Step 15

15 Fit the right-side facing-out pair of pants into the wrong-side facing-out pair of pants so that their right sides are together, and align their top edges, side seams, and center seams.

16 Using a ¼" seam allowance, sew the two pairs together all around the top edge, and finish by overlapping your beginning stitches. Pull the pairs away from each other so that the ankles are opposite each other, and then reach through one leg to pull the other pair through and out so that you can turn them right side out with their wrong sides together.

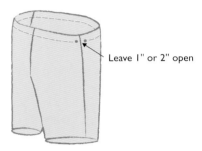

Leave 1" or 2" open

Step 17

Create the Waistband

17 Smooth and press the top waist seam well. To create an elastic channel, sew a seam through both layers, beginning at one side seam and continuing around the waist line at a healthy ⅝" from the top folded edge, stop your stitch line about an inch or two away from where you began, and backstitch.

18 Using the length of elastic for your specified size, feed the elastic through one end of the channel and out the other by reaching in between the two layers of pants. Use either a large safety pin or a bodkin, whichever you like.

NOTE: It's a good idea to first check the elastic length around the baby's waist, if possible. It should be taut, but not constricting.

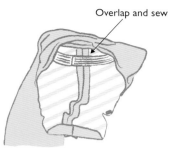

Overlap and sew

Step 19

19 After removing the safety pin and making sure your elastic isn't flipped, overlap the ends of the elastic by about an inch and sew them together with a few rows of stitching back and forth. You need to pull the top layer of pants up out of your way, and also stretch each end of elastic out of the channel to do this, which is a little cumbersome, so be patient.

20 Continue to work with the joined elastic and waistband channel to get it fully into place. You can then close the line of channel stitching from Step 17 by picking up where you left off and overlapping the beginning stitches. Press well.

Finish the Trousers

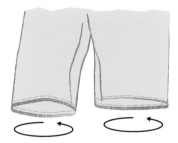

Topstitch around ankle

Step 21

21 With wrong sides together, work with the outer and reverse layers to align the creased bottom edges at each ankle, matching the side seams and the inseams. Pin in place and then topstitch around each ankle to sew the layers together using a scant ⅛" seam allowance. Press well. Fold up the cuffs from either side as desired.

NOTE: The following instructions are only needed if you will be making the elastic either smaller or larger to custom fit the size of the waistband.

—Patchwork
Sleeping Sack—

Patchwork Sleeping Sack

*I*t seems as soon as you've perfected your swaddling style, that baby has wiggled out of swaddling altogether. This sleeping sack is a perfect way to keep baby safely warm during sleep time, night or day. The patchwork front offers the sweet, cozy look of a quilt, and using cotton flannel for the lining adds a layer of warmth and softness. The particular style of patchwork that you make for the front is completely up to you. You can even choose to repurpose an existing quilt top. Once baby has outgrown this sack, you could again repurpose much of the patchwork front for another quilted project. You will continue to chase your baby's growing size for years to come, so enjoy this small size while you can.

Materials

Patchwork rectangle, 20" width × 24" length for Front Panel

¾ yard cotton for outer sides

I yard cotton flannel for lining

½ yard of ½"-wide Velcro

Cotton fabric for a 2-yard length of 2"-wide bias binding

Patchwork Sleeping Sack pattern pieces inside the pocket

> **Finished Dimensions:**
> **6 weeks–3 mos** Chest: 25", Length: 22" (Follow suggestions within pattern cutting directions to make a larger size sleeping sack.)

My Color Notes

Tiny little Claire deserved a little patchwork as sweet and soft as she is. These 2" cotton voile squares are made from various shades of pink, red, and magenta with shots here and there of gold and plum. The linings and back piece are made from a paler pink printed cotton flannel for added warmth.

Trace and Cut

I   Trace and cut pattern pieces **A, A continued, B, B continued, C,** and **C continued** from pattern page 5. Make sure to include the dotted join lines on the Front

Panel (**A**), then lay the tracing paper over (**A continued**), letting the dotted join lines overlap, and continue to trace so that you have a complete piece of the Front Panel. Mark the Velcro tab positions.

2   Repeat Step I with the Under Panel (**B**) and (**B continued**) so that you have a complete piece of the Under Panel.

3   Repeat Step I with the Back Panel (**C**) and (**C continued**) so that you have a complete piece of the Back Panel.

NOTE: If you'd like to make a sleeping sack that is better sized for babies from 3–5 months, just add an equal amount of length to pieces A, B, and C. Most babies will fit just fine in the width of the sleeping sack for several months, but if you'd like to add a little width, do so equally on the side seams of the Front Panels, the Under Panels, and the Back Panel.

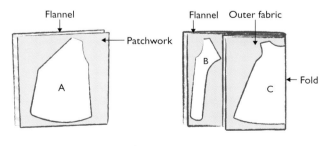

Steps 4, 5, and 6

4 Lay wrong sides of the patchwork rectangle and lining flannel together, and cut one Front Panel (**A**) from both pieces at the same time.

5 Lay wrong sides of the outer fabric and lining flannel together, and cut one Under Panel (**B**) from both pieces at the same time.

6 Lay wrong sides of the outer fabric and lining flannel together, and then fold and cut one Back Panel (**C**) on the fold from both pieces at the same time.

7 Cut enough 2"-wide bias strips so that once joined, the total length is approximately 2 yards (45") long.

8 On the right side of the Front Panel lining, mark the placement for the Velcro tabs.

9 On the right side of the outer Under Panel, mark the placement for the Velcro tabs.

Sew the Outer Panels

10 With right sides together and using a ⅝" seam allowance, sew the patchwork Front Panel to the outer Back Panel at the shoulder seam.

11 With right sides together and using a ⅝" seam allowance, sew the outer Under Panel to the outer Back Panel at the shoulder seam. Press both shoulder seams open.

12 Repeat Steps 8 and 9 with the three lining pieces.

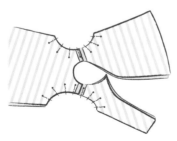

Step 13

13 With right sides together and aligning shoulder seams and like pieces, lay the joined outer pieces with the joined lining pieces and pin together around the armholes.

14 Use a ⅝" seam allowance to sew the joined outer pieces to the joined lining pieces along the curve of the armholes at both sides. Clip the curved seam allowances on both sides, turn right side out, and press.

Assemble the Front and Back Panels

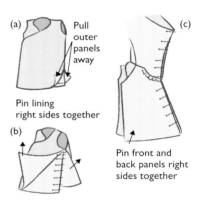

(a) Pull outer panels away

Pin lining right sides together

(b)

(c)

Pin front and back panels right sides together

Step 15

15 Lay out the joined front and back with the right sides of the outer Front Panel and outer Under Panel facing up. (a) Separate the bottom side corner of the outer Front Panel from the Front Panel lining, and pin the Front Panel lining together with the Back Panel lining with right sides together. (b) Continue to pull the outer Front Panel and the outer Back Panel away from their linings so that you can pin the side seam of the Front Panel lining and the Back Panel lining together all the way up to the armhole seam. Be sure to match the lining and outer armhole seams together. (c) Turn the Front Panel and Back Panel completely up toward each other with their right sides together, and pin them from their bottom corners, along the side seam all the way to the armhole.

16 With right sides together and using a ⅜" seam allowance, sew the Front Panel to the Back Panel and the Front Panel lining to the Back Panel lining in one continuous side seam, stopping at the armhole with the needle down in the armhole seam, to take a bit of a turn to continue sewing to the bottom edge of the linings. Press the outer and lining side seam allowances open. Then lay the outer and lining wrong sides together again and press from both sides.

17 Repeat Steps 15 and 16 with the outer Under Panel, Back Panel, and the Under Panel lining and Back Panel lining at the other side seam.

Step 18

18 Machine-baste the outer panels together with the lining panels on all unfinished edges using a ¼" seam allowance as shown in the figure above, matching the side seams with the lining side seams.

19 Just to the outer side of the basting line from Step 18, also zigzag-stitch the edges, starting at the top center point of the Under Panel and continuing down toward the bottom, around all bottom edges, and finishing at the bottom corner of the Front Panel.

20 With right sides together and using a ½" seam allowance, join as many 2"-wide bias strips as necessary to make a strip approximately 45" long. Use 45-degree angled seams in the strip so that you are sewing on the grain of the fabric. Trim the seam allowances and press them open.

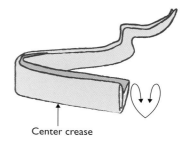

Center crease

Step 21

21 Fold the bias strip in half lengthwise with wrong sides together, and press a crease down the middle. Then fold in each of the side edges to the wrong side and to meet the crease, and press two more creases. The final strip should be a triple-folded bias tape that is approximately ½" wide. Trim one end to blunt the edge.

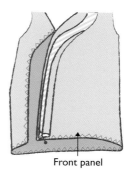

Front panel

Step 22

22 With right sides together, place the blunt end of the bias tape at the bottom corner of the Front Panel, and after unfolding the bias tape, align it with the panel edge and pin them in place.

23 Using a ½" seam allowance, begin sewing the bias tape to the inner edge of the Front Panel. This seam line should fall directly into one of the pressed creases. Continue sewing around the neckline until you are a few inches away from the center point edge of the Under Panel, and then stop with your needle down.

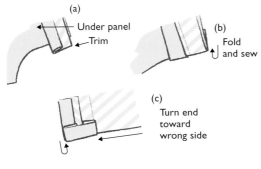

(a)
Under panel
Trim

(b)
Fold
and sew

(c)
Turn end
toward
wrong side

Step 24

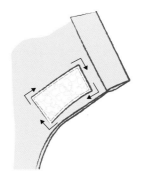

Step 28

24 (a) Trim the bias tape to be just about ¾" past the edge of the Under Panel center point. (b) Fold and wrap the right side of the bias tape around to the lining side, and continue sewing to the edge of the Under Panel to include this fold. (c) Turn the bias tape end right-side out and then tuck the end toward its wrong side.

25 Wrap the bias around the edge of the seam allowance and keep the folds in place so that the raw edges of the bias tape are concealed. Pin in place all along the binding edge.

26 I recommend hand-sewing the bias binding in place on the lining side by making a blind stitch through the binding and seam allowances just as you would with a quilt binding. If, however, you would like to machine-sew the binding, do so with the folded edge of the binding right up against the edge of the binding seam on the lining side and topstitch through all layers, keeping a consistent ⅛" distance from the binding seam. Press well.

27 Cut both the hook and loop sides of the Velcro into six 1½" lengths. Pin the hook sides of the Velcro to the marked positions on the right side of the Under Panel. Pin the loop sides of the Velcro to the marked positions on the lining side of the Front Panel.

28 Sew each of the Velcro pieces in place by making a rectangular seam around the outermost edges of each Velcro piece on the Under Panel and the Front Panel.

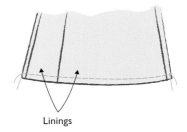

Linings

Step 29

29 Close all the Velcro tabs and keep them closed as you turn the sleeping sack inside out so that the lining side is facing out.

30 Make sure the side seams are in line with the side folds, and then sew the Front and Under Panels to the Back Panel using a ⅝" seam allowance through all layers along the bottom edge of the sleeping sack. Turn it right side out, smooth out the bottom seam, and press well.

31 I added a few traditional quilting details by making hand-quilting stitches around the armholes and all along the inner sides of the binding about ¼" away from the edges and seam lines.

-Pretty-as-a-Picture Dress-

Pretty-as-a-Picture Dress

*F*avorite fabrics, like favorite photos, deserve to be framed. Maybe you've been saving something gorgeous deep in your fabric stacks for the chance to show it off in this precious little baby-girl frock. This is also a perfect opportunity to use a vintage quilt block, handkerchief, or embroidered linen as center stage in this dress. The bodice and skirt are styled and pieced together so that they will frame a favorite square of fabric both front and back. A crossover front and an elastic waist make it very comfy so that getting dressed is as simple as getting a squirmy little sweetie dressed could be.

Materials

Light- to medium-weight woven cotton fabric:

- ¾ yard for main fabric (top and skirt framing)
- ⅓ yard for feature fabric

½ yard lightweight cotton voile for lining

½ yard of ¼"-wide elastic

Pretty-as-a-Picture Dress pattern pieces inside the pocket

Finished Dimensions:

0–3 mos Chest: 21", Length: 15" **3–6 mos** Chest: 21", Length: 16" **6–9 mos** Chest: 22½", Length: 17" **9–12 mos** Chest: 23", Length: 18" **12–18 mos** Chest: 24", Length: 19" **18–24 mos** Chest: 25", Length: 19½"

My Color Notes

Carrie is so bright-eyed and curious, and I thought her dress should make use of these bright and clever prints. Using clear, deep colors I chose the framing fabric color to pick up the central magenta flower on my feature fabric. Turning the stripe sideways on the side panels adds interest to a simple pattern.

Trace and Cut

1 Trace and cut the following pieces in your desired size on pattern sheet 7, making sure to transfer all of the markings: Front Bodice (**A**), Back Bodice (**B**), and Side Panels (**E**).

Measure and Cut

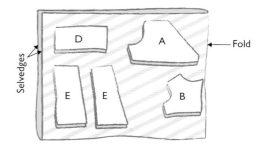

Steps 2, 3, 4, and 5

2 Draft the following pieces based on your desired size:

- Center Panel (**C**) should measure 8¾" square, for all sizes

- Bottom Panel (**D**) should be a rectangle in one of the following sizes based on length:

  0–3 months: 2½" × 8¾"

  3–6 months: 4" × 8¾"

6–9 months: 4¾" × 8¾"

9–12 months: 5½" × 8¾"

12–18 months: 6⅛" × 8¾"

18–24 months: 6⅞" × 8¾"

3 Fold the main fabric with right sides together and cut Front Bodice (**A**) so that you are left with two pieces that are cut opposite. Mark the overlap dots on the right side of the fabric on both Front Bodice pieces.

4 Place the fold line edge of the Back Bodice (**B**) on the main fabric fold and cut one Back Bodice piece.

5 Cut Bottom Panel (**D**) from the folded main fabric so that you end with two pieces.

6 Cut Side Panels (**E**) twice from the folded main fabric so that you are left with four pieces (two that are cut opposite the other two). Mark the side seam edges on the right side of the fabric on all four pieces.

7 Cut two Center Panels (**C**) from your feature fabric.

8 Fold the lining fabric with right sides together and cut Front Bodice (**A**) so that you are left with two pieces that are cut opposite.

9 Place the fold line edge of the Back Bodice (**B**) on the lining fabric fold and cut one Back Bodice piece.

Sew the Bodices

Step 10

10 With right sides together, using a ⅝" seam allowance and making sure the pointed ends of the Front Bodices are overlapping each other, sew each of the Front Bodice pieces to the Back Bodice at the shoulder seams. Press the seams open.

11 Repeat Step 10 with the Front Bodice lining and the Back Bodice lining.

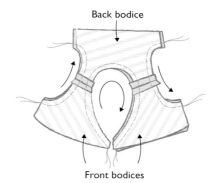

Back bodice

Front bodices

Step 12

12 With right sides together, align all edges of the joined Front and Back Bodices with the joined Front and Back Bodice linings. Using a ⅝" seam allowance, sew the necklines together from the pointed edge of one side of the Front Bodice, all around the back neckline and to the pointed edge of the other Front Bodice. Also with a ⅝" seam allowance, sew along both of the curved armhole edges. Clip all curved seam allowances, turn right side out (by reaching between the Back Bodice layers to pull each Front Bodice through its shoulder seam), smooth the seams with your fingers, and then press well.

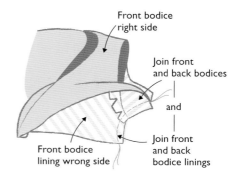

Front bodice
right side

Join front
and back bodices

and

Join front
and back
bodice linings

Front bodice
lining wrong side

Step 13

13 Lay the joined bodices and bodice linings so that the overlapped front is facing up. At the bottom-side corner of one of the Front Bodices, pull it up away from its lining and do the same with the Back Bodice directly behind at the same corner, thereby turning the right sides of the Front and Back Bodices toward each other. Align the armhole seams with seam allowances kept down toward the wrong side of the linings and, using a ⅝" seam allowance, sew the side seam from the bottom corner of the Front and Back Bodices to the bottom corner of the Front and Back Bodice linings. (You need to stop this stitch line with your needle down in the armhole seam in order to lift the foot and turn the pieces to continue down the side seam of the linings.)

14 Make a clip in the seam allowance pointing to the armhole seam. Press the seam allowances open and then fold the bodices and linings back together so that the side seam allowances are against each other. Press from the outside and lining side.

15 Repeat Steps 13 and 14 at the other side of the Front and Back Bodices and linings.

16 Overlap the lined Front Bodices so that the end points on each side meet the pattern's overlap dots and the bottom edges are in line with one another. Using a ½" seam allowance, machine-baste the Front Bodices together where they overlap. Set aside.

17 With right sides together and using a ⅝" seam allowance, sew the Bottom Panel to the side of the Center Panel that you want at the bottom edge. Then zigzag the seam allowance edges together and press down toward the wrong side of the Bottom Panel.

Assemble the Skirt

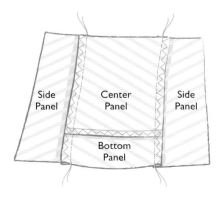

Step 18

18 With right sides together and using a ⅝" seam allowance, sew the Side Panel to the joined Center and Bottom Panels (be sure you are sewing the edge of the Side Panel that is *NOT* marked as the side seam). Then zigzag the seam allowance edges together and press toward the wrong side of the Side Panel. Repeat with the other Side Panel on the other side of the Center and Bottom Panels. This is now the Skirt Front.

19 Repeat Steps 17 and 18 with the remaining skirt panels to create the Skirt Back.

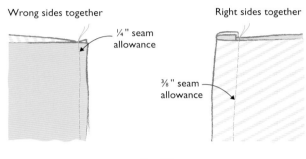

Step 20

20 The Skirt Front and Back will be joined with French seams. Begin by sewing the skirt *WRONG* sides together using a ¼" seam allowance at both side seams. Press the seam allowances to one side. Then turn the wrong side out so that the right sides are together, and sew both of the side seams once more using a ⅜" seam allowance, thereby encasing the first seam within the second. Press the seam allowance to one side, and then press the seams from the skirt's right side.

21 Starting at one side, machine-baste the top edge of the Side Panels only, both front and back in one continuous stitch line, using a ½" seam allowance, leaving plenty of top thread and bobbin slack at the beginning and end of the stitching. (You will begin and end this basting line at the seam between the Center Panels and the Side Panels on each side.)

22 Tug on the top thread at one end of the basting stitches to pull up the bobbin thread from underneath, and knot them together.

23 Repeat Steps 21 and 22 on the other side of the skirt.

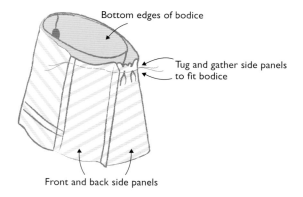

Bottom edges of bodice

Tug and gather side panels to fit bodice

Front and back side panels

Step 24

24 Turn the skirt inside out and place the bodice inside the skirt. With right sides together, align the skirt's upper edges with the bottom edges of the bodice, also matching side seams. Tug on the loose bobbin threads from the side basting lines to draw up and gather the sides. Continue to do this equally on both sides until you've reduced the size of the skirt enough to fit against the size of the bodice perfectly. Knot the loose ends of both of the basting threads. Pin the skirt to the bodice.

Attach the Skirt and Finish the Dress

25 With right sides together and using a ⅝" seam allowance, sew the top edges of the skirt to the bottom edges of the bodice all around the circumference of the waistline, and finish by overlapping your beginning stitches. Trim the seam allowances down to about ¼".

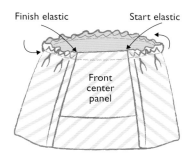

Finish elastic   Start elastic

Front center panel

Step 26

26 You'll now be adding elastic to the waistline seam allowance that was created in the previous step. The elastic will go around the entire waistline with the exception of the front Center Panel section of the dress. So begin anchoring the ¼" elastic with a few zigzag stitches onto the seam allowance, beginning at the seam between the Center Panel and a Side Panel of the Skirt Front. Then continue to sew the elastic to the seam allowance using a zigzag stitch and stretching the elastic taut as it passes under the needle. Finish at the other seam between the Center Panel and Side Panel of the Skirt Front with a backstitch. Trim off the excess elastic at the end.

27 Fold the dress bodice back up, and press the waistline seam allowance up toward the lining side of the bodice. Press well from inside and outside of the dress. You may choose to tack the seam allowances up against the bodice at the sides by stitching in the ditch of the side seams (right into the seams) with a few back-and-forth stitches.

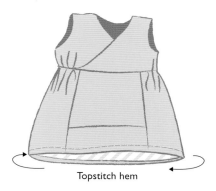

Topstitch hem

Step 28

28 Fold the bottom edge of the dress skirt ¼" toward the wrong side and press a crease. Roll the folded edge once more ¼" toward the wrong side and topstitch a hem with a ⅛" seam allowance. Press well.

-Baby-in-the-Hood Jacket-

Baby-in-the-Hood Jacket

*T*hough this baby project requires a few more steps than the rest, I think you'll find the time so worth it once you're finished. Seeing sweet baby eyes and cheeks peek out of the hood is just irresistible. Cut to fit comfortably over other clothing and also leave a little wiggle room, the jacket has plenty of darling details. The button placket, button loops, and the hood's stripe are all fun opportunities to play around with your favorite fabrics. Because the jacket is fully lined, turning up the sleeve cuffs before baby grows into it completely shows off a bit of cute contrast, too. You will, without a doubt, have the best-dressed baby in the hood.

Materials

Lightweight woven cotton fabric:

- ¾ yard for main fabric
- ¾ yard for lining fabric
- ½ yard for accent fabric (Button Placket and Hood Stripe)

Strip of fabric 1" wide × 16" long for Button Loops

4 buttons, ¾" diameter

16–20" of ¼"-wide elastic, depending on jacket size

Lightweight fusible interfacing for Button Placket

Baby-in-the-Hood Jacket pattern pieces inside the pocket

Finished Dimensions:

0–3 mos Chest: 21", Length: 10¼" **3–6 mos** Chest: 22", Length: 10¾" **6–9 mos** Chest: 22¾", Length: 11" **9–12 mos** Chest: 23½", Length: 11¼" **12–18 mos** Chest: 24¼", Length: 11½" **18–24 mos** Chest: 25", Length: 11¾"

My Color Notes

Reuben's gorgeous face reminds me of vintage baby photos from the forties and fifties so I styled his jacket accordingly. The little yellow diamond-checks feel very mid-century modern and the blue flannel contrast print for the placket

and hood sparkle just like his sweet baby blues. I lined the jacket with a deeper grey and blue flannel print that also has some gold elements to tie it all together.

Trace and Cut

1   Trace and cut the following pieces from pattern page 6 in your desired size: Front (**A**), Back (**B**), Sleeve (**C**), Button Placket (**D**), Placket Interfacing (**d**), Hood (**E**), and Hood Stripe (**F**). Be sure to transfer all notches and markings to your pattern pieces.

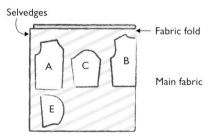

Steps 2, 3, 4, and 5

2   Fold the main jacket fabric with right sides together, and cut Front (**A**) once so that you end with two Front pieces that are cut opposite each other. Mark the hood placement diamond.

3 Place the fold line edge of the Back (**B**) on the main fabric fold and cut Back piece.

4 Cut Sleeve (**C**) once from the folded main fabric so that you end up with two Sleeve pieces.

5 Cut Hood (**E**) once from the folded main fabric so that you end up with two Hood pieces that are cut opposite each other. Mark the "neck edge" on the Hood pieces.

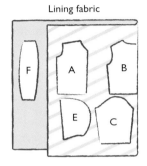

Lining fabric

Steps 6, 7, 8, 9, and 10

6 Cut one Hood Stripe (**F**) from the lining fabric, and mark the "neck edge."

7 Fold the lining fabric with right sides together and cut Front (**A**) once so that you end up with two Front lining pieces that are cut opposite each other.

8 Place the fold line edge of the Back (**B**) on the lining fabric fold and cut one Back piece.

9 Cut two Sleeves (**C**) from the folded lining fabric so that you end up with two Sleeve lining pieces.

10 Cut one Hood (**E**) from the folded lining fabric so that you end up with two Hood lining pieces that are cut opposite each other. Mark the "neck edge" on the Hood lining pieces.

11 Cut two Button Placket (**D**) pieces from the accent fabric.

12 Cut one Hood Stripe (**F**) piece from the accent fabric, and mark the "neck edge."

13 Cut two Placket Interfacing pieces (**d**) from the lightweight fusible interfacing.

14 Cut the ¼"-wide elastic in one of the following lengths based on size:

0–3 months: 16"	9–12 months: 18½"
3–6 months: 17"	18 months: 19"
6–9 months: 18"	24 months: 19½"

Construct the Hood

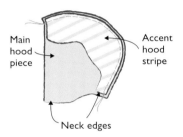

Main hood piece

Accent hood stripe

Neck edges

Step 15

15 With right sides together and using a ½" seam allowance, sew the accent Hood Stripe to one of the main Hood pieces, also making sure to match single notches. Clip the curved seam allowances and press them toward the wrong side of the Hood Stripe.

16 Topstitch on the Hood Stripe side of the seam ¼" from the seam, sewing through all the seam allowances.

17 Repeat Steps 15 and 16 to join the remaining main Hood piece to the other side of the accent Hood Stripe.

18 Repeat Steps 14–16 with the two Hood lining pieces and the Hood Stripe lining.

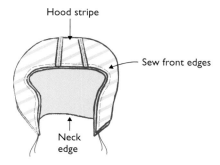

Hood stripe

Sew front edges

Neck edge

Step 19

19 Fit the main Hood to the Hood lining with right sides together, aligning all edges. Sew the front edges together from one corner to the other using a ¼" seam allowance. Turn the right sides out, and press well.

20 Sew an elastic channel along the front edge of the Hood by topstitching ⅝" from the edge through the main and lining layers with wrong sides together from one front corner to the other.

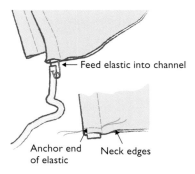

Feed elastic into channel

Anchor end of elastic   Neck edges

Step 21

21 Using the appropriate length of ¼"-wide elastic for your particular size jacket, use a bodkin or a large safety pin to feed the elastic through the channel at the front of the Hood. Once the end of the elastic is just barely peeking out of the channel where you started, anchor the elastic in place by backstitching a few times over it just about ¼" from the neck edge of the Hood.

22 Finish feeding the elastic through the channel and out the other side, and anchor the opposite end of the elastic as you did in Step 21.

23 Machine-baste the Hood and Hood lining together using a ¼" seam allowance along the aligned neck edges from one corner to the other. Set aside.

Sew the Main Jacket and Lining

24 With right sides together and using a ½" seam allowance, sew the shoulders of the main Back to the shoulders of both main Front pieces, making sure the center edges of the Front pieces are at the center. Press the seam allowances open.

NOTE: The Sleeve is the same shape at the front as it is at the back, so there is no need to differentiate between a right and a left sleeve as you prepare to sew them to the armholes.

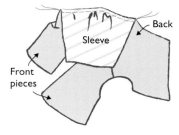

Back

Sleeve

Front pieces

Step 25

25 With right sides together and using a ½" seam allowance, sew one main Sleeve to the armhole of the joined main Front and Back pieces. Take care to ease the curve of the Sleeve onto the armhole. Clip the curved seam allowances and press toward the wrong sides of the joined Front and Back.

26 On the right side of the armhole, topstitch on the Front/Back side of the armhole seam ¼" from the seam, going through all seam allowances. Press well.

27 Repeat Steps 25 and 26 with the remaining main Sleeve at the other armhole.

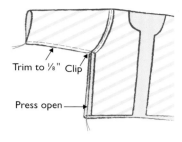

Trim to ⅛" Clip

Press open

Step 28

28 With right sides together, aligning the armhole seam, and using a ½" seam allowance, sew the Front to the Back starting at the cuff of the Sleeve and ending at the bottom edge of the Front and Back side seam. Clip the seam allowance toward the armhole seam and press the side seam allowances open. Trim the Sleeve seam allowances to ⅛" and press to one side. Press the seam open.

29 Repeat Step 28 on the other side to complete the side seam.

30 Fold each Sleeve cuff ½" toward the wrong side and press a crease.

31 Repeat Steps 24–30 with the Front lining pieces and the Back lining.

Finish the Jacket

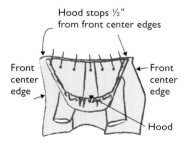

Hood stops ½" from front center edges

Front center edge

Front center edge

Hood

Step 32

32 Find and mark the center point of the Hood's neck edge by folding it in half. Find and mark the center of the main Back's neckline. With the main side of the Hood against the right side of the main jacket, align the neck

edge of the Hood with the neckline of the jacket, also aligning their center back points, and pin together. The front edges of the Hood match the front at the diamond marks.

33 Machine-baste the Hood to the main jacket using a ⅜" seam allowance from the center edge of one Front piece to the other.

34 With right sides of the jacket lining and main jacket together, sandwiching the Hood in between them, align and pin their neckline edges, also making sure that their Front piece top corners are aligned. Then using a ½" seam allowance, sew through all layers along the neckline from the center edges of the Front on one side to the other. Clip the seam allowances.

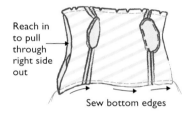

Reach in to pull through right side out

Sew bottom edges

Step 35

35 Keeping the lining and main jacket right sides together, sew their bottom edges together using a ½" seam allowance from the center edges of the Front on one side to the other. Be sure to keep the hood and the sleeves out of your way as you sew the bottom seam. Reach through the Front center edges on one side to pull the jacket through and turn it right side out.

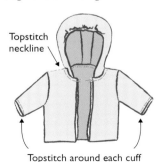

Topstitch neckline

Topstitch around each cuff

Steps 36 and 37

36 Once you have the jacket turned right side out, insert the Sleeve linings into the main sleeves and work with them until they fit together well, their seams are matched, and their creased cuffs are aligned. Topstitch each sleeve lining to its Sleeve around the cuffs using a ¼" seam allowance.

37 Smooth and press the neckline well from both sides of the jacket, and then topstitch the neckline on the Front/Back side of the neckline seam ¼" away from the seam. Press well.

38 With wrong sides together, fold the 16" × 1" strip of fabric for the Button Loops in half lengthwise and press a crease. Then fold in each of the long edges ¼" toward the wrong side until their edges meet at the center crease, fold them over each other, and press once more. You should be left with a ¼"-wide folded strip that has its raw edges concealed. Topstitch through all layers. Then cut the length into four 4"-long pieces.

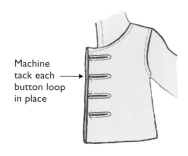

Machine tack each button loop in place

Step 39

39 Refer to the Front piece pattern to mark the Button Loop positions on the front left for a boy or the front right for a girl. Fold each loop in half, and center them over each mark, with their edges aligned with the center edge of the Front, and pin each in place. Machine-tack each Button Loop in place by backstitching a few times through all layers, including the jacket lining.

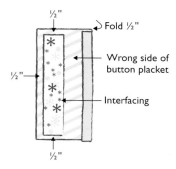

Steps 40 and 41

40 With the fusible side of one of the Placket Interfacings against the wrong side of one of the Button Plackets, position the interfacing so that it is ½" away from three of the Button Placket edges, as shown in the figure above. Press with an iron to fuse in place. (Be sure to follow the directions for your specific type of lightweight fusible interfacing.) Repeat with the remaining Button Placket and Placket Interfacing.

41 On the long side of the Button Placket that is farther from the interfacing, fold the edge ½" back toward the wrong side and press a crease. Repeat with the remaining Button Placket.

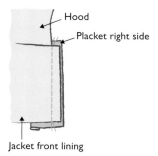

Step 42

42 With right sides together, align one of the Button Plackets (the edge that is *NOT* creased) with one of the Front center edges, letting the Button Placket extend ½" beyond the top and bottom finished edges of the jacket Front. Using a ½" seam allowance, sew the Button Placket to the Front edge, sewing also through the lining layer.

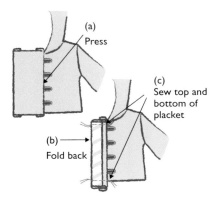

(a)
Press

(c)
Sew top and
bottom of
placket

(b) →
Fold back

Step 43

43 (a) Fold the wrong side of the Button Placket toward the seam allowances and press. (b) Fold the Button Placket again so that the right sides are together and the creased edge meets the seam line from Step 42. (c) Sew the top edge of the folded Button Placket layers together using a ½" seam allowance. Also sew the bottom edge of the folded Button Placket layers together using a ½" seam allowance. Then turn the Button Placket right side out and press.

44 Topstitch the Button Placket on the Button Placket side of the seam ¼" from the seam line and going through all layers so that the creased edge of the Button Placket is concealing the seam allowances on the inside of the jacket. (If you are on the side of the jacket that has the Button Loops, pin them against the Button Placket so that they are also caught in the topstitching line.)

45 Repeat Steps 42–44 with the remaining Button Placket on the other Front edge of the jacket.

46 Hand-sew each of the four buttons in place on the Button Placket that is opposite the Button Loop side. Align them with each of the Button Loops to establish their position.

Family Sewing

−Patchwork Welcome Notes−

We are so overjoyed and thankful
to announce the birth of our son

Roman Ambrose Horner

who arrived on May 19, 2009
weighing 7lbs 5.75 oz
& measuring 20.5 inches long

He joins his adoring siblings
Juliana, Nicolas, Joseph, Isabela, and Eleni

With love, Anna Maria & Jeff Horner

Patchwork Welcome Notes

*W*ell, this is the first of the Family Sewing projects. However, I'm going to skip the sewing part. These handmade birth announcements have a miniature patchwork quilt that folds right over a picture of your precious new bundle. Only, this patchwork is created by first making little fabric "stickers" and then composing them onto printed announcement cards. This is a wonderful project for the tiniest scraps in your sewing room, and the smallest hands in your house, too. Let older siblings or even some cousins help with this project. They will remember the time that you spent working on these together, and it helps make them feel like they are part of this new beginning in your family. Also, you could likely use the help if you've just brought a new baby home, although some of the required tasks, such as the cutting and the ironing, are best suited for an adult or older sibling. Think of this project as a family activity with the bonus of checking a to-do off your list.

Materials

Printed or digital photo of your new baby

Computer with photo-editing software (optional)

Color or photo printer (optional)

8½" × 11" heavy-weight, matte printer paper (each page will yield two announcements)

Woven cotton fabric scraps

Steam-A-Seam fusible web (9" × 12" sheets)

X-Acto or other craft knife

Finished Dimensions: 4¼" × 6½"

My Color Notes

This is one project where it is perfectly acceptable to use up all of your scraps regardless of color or print. You may chose to cater your colors to what gender the baby being announced happens to be.

Print the Announcement

1   Choose a photo of your baby that is a simple headshot, perhaps with her arms and shoulders visible, too. If you don't have one already, you might try taking a photo of her lying on a solid-colored blanket on the floor as you stand over the baby to get an aerial view (keep that camera strap around your neck for safety). Once you've chosen a photo, upload it to your computer and open it in your desired software. You might try cropping the photo with photo-editing software so that it will work well in the layout detailed in the next few steps.

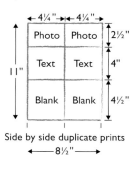

Side by side duplicate prints

Step 2

2   The previous figure and the following description detail the dimensions of each inside area of the printed announcement that you can go by to compose the file in your computer (keep in mind that if you'd like to take this layout to a printer to process the printed portion of the project, this is the information they'll need to know):

- The 8½" × 11" page should first be divided in half down the length so that each announcement space is 4¼" × 11".

- Within the 4¼" × 11" space, the top photo area should be 4¼" wide and 2½" tall.

- Directly below the photo space, there should be text space that is 4¼" wide and 4" tall.

- The remaining space below the text area can be filled with color, a pattern, more text, another photo, or left blank.

3   Once you've made one layout in the 4¼" × 11" dimensions as detailed above, you can copy and paste the same exact format beside the first, so that each sheet that you print will have two announcements that you will separate by cutting (in a later step).

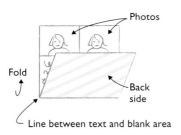

Step 4

4   Print one sheet out to test your dimensions and image size settings. Fold the bottom edge of the test print up toward the photo with the crease between the text area and the lower blank area (which is 6½" from the top). Check to be sure you can see baby's face peeking out from the folded-over flap. If not, you many need to readjust the photo size and placement so that baby's face will be at least partially visible.

5   Once you've tested the printout and made any necessary adjustments to the file, print half as many sheets as the total number of announcements that you'll need (for example, if you need 24 announcements, print 12 sheets).

Patchwork the Announcement

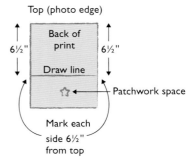

Step 6

6   On the back side of each sheet, measure 6½" from the top (baby photo edge being the top) on each side and make a mark. Draw a light pencil line from one mark across to the other. The area below the pencil line is the area that you'll be patchworking. Draw this line on the back side of the remaining prints. If you've got kids helping, you might also want to draw a star or some mark in the patchwork space for them to remember.

7   Choose several different fabric scraps (which don't have to be any bigger than a postcard) and press them well.

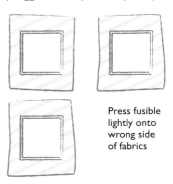

Step 8

8 Cut the 9" × 12" sheets of Steam-A-Seam crosswise and lengthwise into four quarters. Peel one of the backing papers off a cut piece of Steam-A-Seam, stick the sticky side onto the wrong side of a fabric scrap, and smooth well. It's fine for now if there are uneven borders of fabric around the fusible web. Continue to do this with all your scraps.

9 Leaving the one backing paper on the fusible web, gently press the scraps with an iron from the right side of the fabric now, to fuse one side of the web to the fabric.

10 Use a straightedge (such as a clear quilt ruler) and a rotary cutter to trim the excess fabric down to the size of the fusible web. Repeat this with all scraps.

11 Use the straightedge and rotary cutter again to cut whatever patchwork shapes you'd like for your "fabric stickers." Evenly sized squares are easy to line up as you compose the patchworks, as are the long, thin strips. Since it's okay to let the fabric pieces overlap a bit or even leave some blank spaces in your patchwork design, make any variety of shapes you'd like. (I'm sure your kids might have some suggestions.)

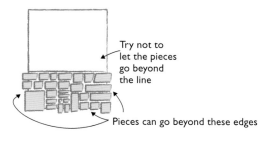

Try not to let the pieces go beyond the line

Pieces can go beyond these edges

Step 12

12 Once you've cut several pieces, you can begin peeling the backing papers of each shape and arranging your quilt pattern on the back of the printed sheets within the designated patchwork space by sticking the wrong side of the fabric right onto the paper. (There is no need to cut the printed announcement sheet into two cards yet, but rather you can patchwork both cards at the same

time on one sheet first.) The shapes stick temporarily with just the press of your fingers and can be removed and repositioned easily. Keep the fabric pieces right up against the line that was drawn in Step 6, but don't worry if pieces run over the other three edges.

13 Once you've filled the patchwork space with fabric pieces, flip the sheet over to the printed side. Use a straightedge and a rotary cutter to trim off all the fabric pieces that extend beyond the edges of the printed sheet. You can save and reuse these scraps for other sheets.

14 After you've trimmed the edges neatly, lay a pressing cloth over the right side of the patchwork area and fuse the patchwork with the iron. Don't overheat the piece— just press lightly.

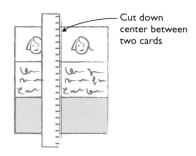

Cut down center between two cards

Step 15

15 You can now cut the sheet into two cards by measuring 4½" from the left side and marking at the top and bottom. Cut from the top mark to the bottom mark, down the center line of the two cards. (This step is best done with an X-Acto or craft knife and straightedge.)

16 Fold the patchwork blanket up over your baby picture. Press the fold well with your fingers to make a good crease, but try not to rub, as it might fray some of the fabrics.

17 Repeat Steps 12–16 to create as many announcements as you wish. Then thank your kids with cookies.

Swaddled Baby Love

*P*reparing for a new baby in your house might mean warming up a certain someone to the idea. In addition to excitement, very often the children you already have might feel a bit of anxiety about having someone else in the house that needs your full attention. I have always noticed that talking to my little ones about the role that they will play as a big brother or sister after baby arrives is an extremely helpful thing to do. And something else that seems to happen without my having to encourage, is my children mirroring everything that I do with the new baby. They even mimic the softer, high-pitched tone of my voice that I use during newborn conversations. I have found them "nursing" their stuffed animals and rocking their "fussy" dolls to sleep countless times. Seeing my own kids' desire to nurture and care for a baby inspired this project. This doll and quilt set will give older siblings a little spring training in swaddling and diapering a baby before it's time for the real thing. Caring for your new little ones side by side, this baby doll might help give your older child someone to focus on while your newborn needs your attention.

Materials

1 yard lightweight cotton muslin for quilt foundation

Various narrow strips of fabric scraps for string-pieced quilt top

1 yard lightweight cotton print for quilt backing

½ yard lightweight cotton for binding

½ yard lightweight cotton for Baby Doll Body in your desired skin-tone shade

¼ yard lightweight white fleece for Diaper(s)

A few inches of sew-on 1"-wide Velcro

Fiberfill stuffing for Baby Doll

Embroidery floss and needle for Baby Doll

Embroidery hoop

Baby Doll pattern pieces inside the pocket

Finished Dimensions:
Quilt: 24" × 24" **Baby:** 7½" × 12"

My Color Notes

Each of my daughters chose their own fabrics for these baby dolls quilts, but I did narrow down the selections for them by first offering a few collections for them to choose from. The string quilt style piecing leaves you with no wrong answers.

Trace and Cut

1   Trace and cut the following pattern pieces from pattern page 3: Baby Doll Body and the Baby Diaper.

2   Cut out as many Baby Diapers from the white fleece as you wish. Set aside.

3   Using a water-soluble fabric marker, trace the Baby Doll Body pieces onto the body fabric, one for the front and one for the back. *DO NOT CUT OUT* at this time. Mark the facial features onto one of the Baby Doll Body pieces. Set them aside.

Cut and Piece the Quilt Top

This particular quilt style is known as a string quilt. For this project, I'm sharing the traditional method of piecing the "strings" onto a layer of foundation fabric. The extra foundation layer eliminates the need for a batting layer and also makes the piecing really easy. If you have a favorite quilt block, feel free to use it in place of these four finished 12" blocks. After making your quilt top, follow the rest of the project starting at Step 18.

4 For the foundation of the four blocks, cut four squares that measure 13" × 13" from the cotton muslin.

5 Cut several strips of fabric scraps (in line with the fabric's grain), ranging from 1" to 2" in width. The beauty of this project is that the strips don't have to have an even thickness, but can be cut at an angle for a kind of bent, cool piecing style.

6 Cut a large square measuring 24½" × 24½" from the backing fabric. Also cut a 10" × 10" square from the backing fabric for the baby pocket.

7 Cut several 4"-wide strips for the bias binding from the binding fabric that will total a length of about 3 yards once joined.

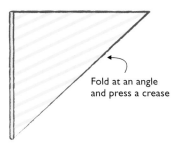

Fold at an angle and press a crease

Step 8

8 To begin a string quilt block, fold one of the foundation squares in half, meeting opposite diagonal points, and press a crease.

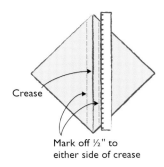

Crease

Mark off ½" to either side of crease

Step 9

9 Open the foundation square out in front of you. Lay a straightedge next to the creased line an equal ½" away all the way down. Make just a couple of marks with a water-soluble fabric pen. Repeat on the other side of the crease. (Making the extra marks to either side of the crease allows you to specifically place the first two center strips on the foundation square in a way that will leave a stripe of the foundation peeking out. If you'd rather just have the whole foundation covered with the fabric strips, you can skip the extra marking steps.)

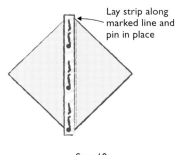

Lay strip along marked line and pin in place

Step 10

10 Lay one of the fabric strips right-side down against the foundation square on top of the crease. Use one of the marked lines as a guide to align the edge of the fabric strip. Let both ends of the strip go beyond the square. Pin the strip in place. (If you'd rather not have the solid, cream-colored stripe of the foundation showing through in the center, just use the crease as a guide for direction.)

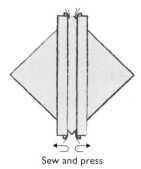

Sew and press

Steps 11 and 12

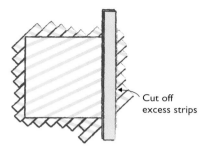

Cut off
excess strips

Step 15

11 Sew the strip to the foundation square ¼" from the edge of the strip that is up against the marked line. Turn the strip to its right side and press.

12 Turn the square around and repeat Steps 10 and 11 so that your block looks like the figure above.

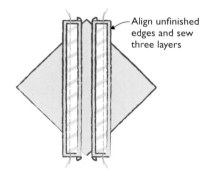

Align unfinished edges and sew three layers

Step 13

13 In the same manner, attach another two strip pieces to the block one at a time, but this time use the unfinished edges of the previous strips as a guide to place the strips in line and sew through all three layers. Fold both strips to their right sides and press.

14 Working your way from the center out, continue to add one strip to each side, and then turn to the right side and press both. Continue in this manner, until you've covered the front of the foundation square.

15 Flip the block over to the bare foundation side and use a straightedge and a rotary cutter to trim off all the excess fabric strips even with the sides of the foundation square.

16 The sewing process could have slightly stretched the foundation square a bit, so flip it to the right strip side, and square up the block by trimming it down to a 12½" square. (If you have the white stripe running across the center, be sure to trim evenly off each side to keep the white stripe in the center diagonal.)

17 Repeat Steps 4–16 three more times so that you have four 12½" square string quilt blocks.

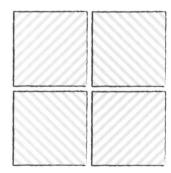

Step 18

18 Arrange the four blocks two by two so that the stripes of the blocks form a diamond shape, as shown above. Rearrange them until you are happy with the balance of light and color.

19 With right sides together and using a ¼" seam allowance, sew the top two squares together. Press the seam allowances open. Repeat with the bottom two squares.

20 Making sure that you have the design aligned correctly, sew the joined top squares to the joined bottom squares with right sides together and using a ¼" seam allowance. Press the seam allowances open. Press the entire quilt top well.

Assemble the Baby Doll Quilt

21 Press ¼" of one edge of the 10" × 10" square baby pocket (cut from the backing fabric) toward the wrong side. Fold another ¼" of the same edge toward the wrong side, and then topstitch through both folds to create a rolled hem. This is the top edge of the pocket.

22 Fold in and press the remaining three edges of the pocket ½" toward the wrong side, and press the creases.

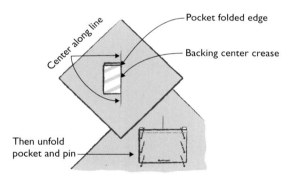

Center along line

Pocket folded edge

Backing center crease

Then unfold pocket and pin

Step 23

23 Fold the quilt backing square in half on the diagonal, and press a crease just in the center area of the diagonal line. Fold the pocket right sides together in half lengthwise, so that you are also folding the top edge in half. Now lay the wrong side of the pocket against the right side of the backing, aligning the folded edge of the pocket with the center diagonal crease of the backing.

You can eyeball centering the pocket on the up and down of the diagonal line. Once you have the pocket in place, unfold it and pin it to the backing, keeping the three creased edges of the pocket folded toward the wrong side.

24 Topstitch the pocket to the backing around the three sides using a ¼" seam allowance. Press well.

25 Lay the quilt top and the backing wrong sides together, aligning all their outer edges. (Trim either layer as necessary so they are the same exact size.) Pin the layers together in several areas. If you care to add any quilting stitches, you should do so now; be sure to not sew them through the back pocket.

26 Attach and finish the binding to the edges by following Steps 31–44 on page 159. Remove the pins and press.

Sew the Baby Doll

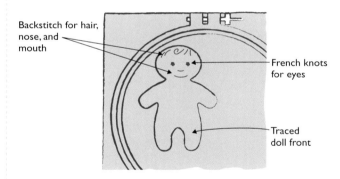

Backstitch for hair, nose, and mouth

French knots for eyes

Traced doll front

Step 27

27 Fit the Baby Doll Body traced fabric into the embroidery hoop to add the facial features. For the eyes, make a small cluster of a few French knots (taught on page 128, Step 27). For the mouth and nose lines, make backstitches (taught on page 103, Steps 7 and 8). You may also want to add some stitched hair lines to the top and back of the baby doll's head. In all instances, remember that the doll will be sewn together with ½" seam allowances, so any stitching closer than that to the edges will not be seen.

28 Remove the Baby Doll Body tracing from the embroidery hoop and carefully cut both the front and the back out of the fabric with scissors on the traced body lines. Be careful not to cut through any of the stitches on the back of the fabric.

Step 29

29 Lay the Baby Doll Body front and back right sides together, aligning all edges, and pin them. Sew the body front to the body back using a ½" seam allowance, taking your time around all of the curves. Leave an opening in the doll's side of about 2–3 inches. Clip all seam allowances.

30 Carefully turn the doll right side out, smoothing out all the curved seams from the inside with your fingers. Turn the open edges toward their wrong sides ½", and press a crease.

31 Stuff the doll with fiberfill using just small amounts at a time, beginning with the head and limbs. Work with the stuffing to make the doll evenly plump but not overstuffed.

32 Close the opening with a blind stitch by hand, using the creases as your guide for the seam.

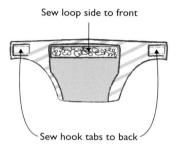

Sew loop side to front

Sew hook tabs to back

Step 33

33 On the right side of the front top edge of the Diaper, sew a length of Velcro (loop side) all along the edge with a straight stitch. Then cut the hook side of the Velcro into two 1" tabs. Sew each of the tabs to the wrong side of the Diaper top-back corners with a straight stitch. Repeat for each Diaper.

Your little one can slide the baby doll into the pocket on the quilt backing for easy swaddling. The pocket is also a nice place to keep extra diapers.

—Family Portrait Tree—

Family Portrait Tree

*L*ife goes quickly, we can all agree. The growth of your family happens in a flash. You're endlessly diapering your child at one stage and then it feels like the very next day that you're visiting colleges together. Making note of the family dynamic while they're all still dangling from the family tree has become increasingly important to me. This project was inspired by both traditional family trees and folk art portraits. The Family Portrait Tree allows you to choose a favorite photo of each family member and transform it into a humble stitched portrait that adorns a fabric tree. Whether you choose to frame your tree, make it the centerpiece of a quilt, or sew it into a pillow, the piece will no doubt become a family heirloom. And depending where you are in your family's growth, you just might choose to leave a few open branches.

Materials

Lightweight cotton muslin for portraits

¾ yard printed cotton fabric for background (smaller or larger, depending on tree size)

¾ yard printed cotton fabric for tree (smaller or larger, depending on tree size)

Printed or digital photo of each family member

Computer with photo-editing software (optional)

Color or photo printer with photo paper (optional)

Tracing paper

Plain white paper

Pencil and black ink pen

Water-soluble fabric pen

Embroidery floss in neutral colors and black

Embroidery needle and hoop

Artist canvas (optional)

Finished Dimensions:
Size will vary depending on your own design.

My Color Notes

I chose some of my favorite small scale vintage style prints so that the designs wouldn't interfere or overpower the stitched portraits. The colors have nothing to do with a landscape or a tree, but simply were chosen based on the décor of the room where we'll hang our family tree.

Compose the Portraits

It's important to keep a few things in mind when choosing which photos you will use as a basis for each family member's portrait. You will want the photo to be as well lit and clear as possible in order to easily make out the features. If you have the photos as digital files and are familiar with your photo-editing software, you can always sharpen the image or heighten the image's contrast to help clarify key features. The size of the photo is up to you, but if the photo is too small, defining facial characteristics becomes a challenge. Most of the photo sizes I used were about 3" × 4" with the face taking up almost the whole picture space. Also be sure that you choose a photo where the entire face and head shape is visible. It's intriguing how much the shape of the head and the curve of an ear can truly define a face at a glance. So you'll want all these details to be clear in your photo so that you have everything available to work with to compose the portraits. Teeth can be a real challenge to depict in a small line drawing and have them look natural. You therefore might choose a pleasant-looking photo before you choose a big smiling photo.

1   Crop and trim the photo print down to the final size or the shape that you would like for your stitched portrait to be. Lay a piece of tracing paper over the portrait, and tape both down to keep them in place.

Step 2

2   Make note of the following facial characteristics on your photo through the tracing paper:

- Eyelids—upper and lower
- Iris shape
- Eyebrows
- Outline of head, jaw, chin, ears, and hairline on the forehead
- Outline of neckline and shoulders
- Shadow lines of nostrils and underneath nose
- Outline of lips—upper and lower
- Any other extreme characteristics such as laugh lines

If the above features are hard to make out through the tracing paper, you may want to trace them right onto the photo with a black ink pen to make them more visible through the tracing paper. Once you can see all the features clearly, begin tracing them onto the tracing paper, first with a pencil. Also trace the square, rectangle, oval, or whatever shape your photo has with a single border line. (I also added a little hand-drawn oval name plate at the center bottom of each portrait border.)

3   When you've traced all the features with a pencil, slide a piece of plain white paper between the tracing paper and the photo so you can have a final look at your drawing. If you need to make some adjustments, erase and keep working until you're happy with it. Once you like the tracing, draw over the pencil lines with the black ink pen.

4   Lay a square of muslin over the ink drawing, and tape both in place. Using the water-soluble marker, trace the drawing and border onto the muslin.

5   Stretch the muslin piece into an embroidery hoop, making sure not to pull it so tightly that you are skewing the drawing in any direction.

6 Separate the six-strand embroidery floss into three strands before threading and knotting your needle; then follow the next steps to make the various stitches.

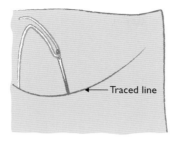

Step 7

7 I used a backstitch to stitch almost all of the lines in my portraits, and a satin stitch in a vertical direction for all of the irises. To start the backstitch, enter the needle from the backside of the fabric and come up right through a drawn line. Make a small stitch back down into the drawn line.

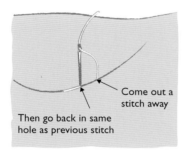

Step 8

8 Come up from the back again and through the drawn line, but this time, come up a stitch distance away from your last stitch. Then enter the needle back into the same hole as the previous stitch. Repeat this continually along your traced lines, with tiny stitches to "draw" the portrait with stitching.

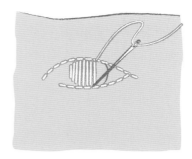

Step 9

9 To create the satin stitch for the iris of the eyes, simply make straight stitches, always entering the fabric's right side from the top of the eye shape and always exiting the fabric's right side at the bottom of the eye shape. Keep your stitches right next to each other.

10 Repeat Steps 1–9 with each of the family portraits and set them aside.

Create the Tree Background

11 Decide on a final size for the background of your family tree. You may want the size to be square, a vertical rectangle, or a horizontal rectangle. No matter the size, be sure to add an inch or two to the size in both directions if you'll be sewing the piece into something like a pillow or quilt. If you plan to wrap the piece around a canvas, take the canvas depth into consideration and add 4" or 5" in both directions to the dimensions of the piece. You could also choose to finish the edges with a hem and have it framed behind glass. Whatever size you want the background piece to be, cut it out now.

12 Cut the printed fabric for the tree in the same size as the background piece.

13 To create a tree image, you can use the Internet to search for a tree silhouette that you like and have it printed in the size you need for tracing. Because photographs of real trees will be quite detailed and time consuming to trace, you may choose to just sketch the general shape of a tree while referring to a favorite tree image. Making a really simple, modern shape for the tree can also be very charming. In any case, trace the tree either freehand or with a cut-out template to the right side of the tree fabric using a water-soluble marker or fabric chalk. Be sure to position the tree onto the fabric in the exact location where you want it to be on the background piece.

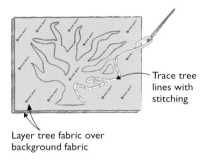

Trace tree lines with stitching

Layer tree fabric over background fabric

Step 14

14 Lay the wrong side of the tree fabric to the right side of the background fabric, aligning all edges. Pin the layers together in several places. Stitch the two layers together with a running stitch or a backstitch along the traced tree lines. (If the tree drawing isn't too complicated, the tree line stitching could also be done with a sewing machine.)

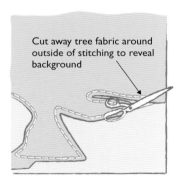

Cut away tree fabric around outside of stitching to reveal background

Step 15

15 Once all the tree lines have been stitched, use a small set of sharp scissors to carefully cut away the tree fabric layer only on the outside of the stitched lines to reveal the background fabric behind. Keep your cut lines about ¼" away from the stitch lines. Continue cutting until the tree silhouette on the background is complete.

Finish the Portrait Tree

16 Cut each of the portraits out of the muslin about ½" away from the stitched borders all around.

17 Use the cutout portraits as templates to cut out (right sides together) a second piece of muslin the same size for each portrait. This will be the backing piece for the portraits.

18 With right sides together and using a ¼" seam allowance, sew the portrait to its backing around all edges. Clip the curved seams and trim the seam allowance corners.

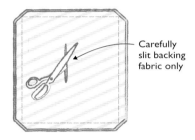

Carefully slit backing fabric only

Step 19

19 Carefully make a slit about an inch or two long in the backing with your scissors. Use a great amount of care to not cut any of the portrait fabric or embroidery stitching in the process.

20 Use this hole in the backing to turn the portrait right side out. Smooth the seams and poke out any corners neatly. Press around the edges.

21 Repeat Steps 18–20 with each of the portraits to finish their edges.

22 Arrange the portraits on the tree background to your liking. Pin them in place. Sew the portraits to the tree and background however you'd like. I made a blind appliqué stitch to attach them, but you could also use your sewing machine or more embroidery stitches.

23 After all of the portraits are sewn to the background, you can complete your piece by sewing it into another project, wrapping it around a canvas and stapling it in the back, or having it professionally framed.

-Dad Bag-

Dad Bag

There is nothing quite so fortunate as sharing your children with a loving and involved father. So many dads run just as many errands, wipe just as many rear-ends, and tote just as much stuff around as moms do. Instead of looking like they're carrying around mom's bag, they deserve a simple style just for them. The Dad Bag is a messenger-style shoulder bag with a straightforward design and slightly more rugged details than the typical baby bag. An easy-to-reach zippered pocket on the outside flap can hold the changing pad and a slim wipe case. A row of elastic loops on the inside can hold a baby bottle, Dad's water bottle, and someone's grape soda, too. The size and shape of the main bag is just enough for a few diapers, some emergency clothes (for baby and Dad), and a blankie. Simply put, it gets the job done without a lot of fuss. Remind you of anyone?

Materials

1½ yards medium- to heavy-weight fabric for outer bag

1½ yards medium-weight fabric for lining (lightweight laminated fabric works well, too)

½ yard cotton quilt batting

½ yard of 22"-wide heavy-duty, double-sided fusible interfacing

¾ yard of 1"-wide elastic

1⅔ yards of 2"-wide sturdy cotton canvas strapping

1 yard of 1"-wide cotton twill tape

2 metal D-rings, 2" wide

1 heavy jacket zipper, approx. 1⅛" wide and 20" long (can be a separating zipper)

1 soup can

Finished Dimensions: 13" × 17" × 3½"

My Color Notes

For Dad, I thought it best to keep the colors on the quieter side, so I went with a very small scale non-typical stripe in tonal blue and gray. The lining is a traditional small scale menswear plaid in a wider assortment of grays and blues. The black and gray used in the strap, zipper, and zipper trim lend a graphic and modern accent.

Trace and Cut

You'll build the Dad Bag pattern using tracing paper, a measuring device, and a soup can. The following steps will make one pattern piece that will be used to create the Outer Front, Outer Back, Lining Front, Lining Back, Outer Flap, Flap Lining, and Pocket Lining.

1   Draw a rectangle on the tracing paper that measures 15" × 18".

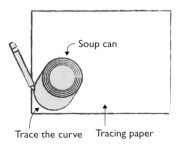

Trace the curve   Tracing paper

Soup can

Step 2

2 On one corner of the rectangle, place the soup can just inside the two edges of the 90-degree corner so that the can is almost touching both of the drawn lines. Trace the shape of the can so that you are creating a curved edge at the corner.

3 Fold the tracing paper rectangle in half on the 18" length, and trace the curved edge onto the opposite corner of the 18" length.

4 Draw an additional 15" line inside the rectangle that is parallel to and 3" away from one of the two 15" sides. This is the zipper line.

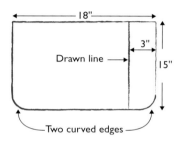

Step 5

5 The above figure shows the details that the bag pattern piece should have, so once you've completed the above steps, you can cut the pattern out of the tracing paper.

6 Using the pattern piece created in the above steps, cut three pieces from the outer bag fabric. These will be the Outer Front, Outer Back, and Outer Flap.

7 Using the same pattern piece, cut four pieces from the lining fabric. These will be the Lining Front and Lining Back, the Flap Lining, and the Pocket Lining.

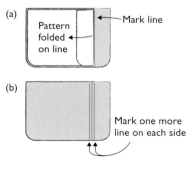

Step 8

8 Fold the pattern piece on the zipper line, and lay it on top of the right side of the Outer Flap and (a) mark the fabric along the folded line with a fabric chalk pencil. (b) Also mark another parallel line to each side of the first line, about ⅜" away from the first line.

9 Cut a strip from the outer fabric measuring 4½" × 45". This will be the Continuous Side.

10 Cut a strip from the lining fabric measuring 4½" × 45". This will be the Continuous Side Lining.

11 Unfold the main pattern piece and draw an inner border that is ½" smaller around the entire perimeter of the pattern. Trim off the border now so that the pattern becomes an inch smaller in both directions. This is now the Back Interfacing pattern.

12 Cut one Back Interfacing using the pattern from Step 11 from the heavy-duty, double-sided fusible interfacing.

13 Cut two lengths of 2"-wide strapping that are 6" long. Set aside the remainder of the strapping.

14 Cut two lengths of 1"-wide twill tapes that are each 15" long.

Sew the Flap

You'll want to use a heavier sewing machine needle, such as a size 16, since you'll be going through several layers and also using heavier materials.

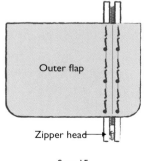

Step 15

15 Place the right side of the zipper against the wrong side of the Outer Flap, centered behind the three chalk lines that you drew in Step 8. Allow the zipper head to extend past the Outer Flap edge, and allow the remaining zipper length to extend past the other Outer Flap edge. (The head of the zipper should be oriented so that it's at the end of the Outer Flap that has the curved edges.) Keeping the zipper teeth in line with the center chalk line (you can do this just by feeling), pin the zipper in place from the fabric's right side on either side of the zipper teeth.

16 From the right side of the fabric, and using a zipper foot, sew the zipper to the fabric, keeping your two stitch lines on the left and right chalk lines to either side of the zipper teeth. (As long as your zipper is wide enough, this should catch the zipper tape on either side just fine.)

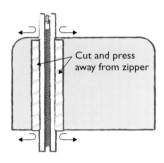

Cut and press away from zipper

Step 17

17 After checking to be sure that the zipper has been sewn on well and centered on the center drawn line, cut the fabric from the right side down the center chalk line. Fold each side of the cut fabric on the stitch line and press the cut edges away from the zipper to either side.

18 Fold each of the 15" lengths of twill tape in half lengthwise, and press a crease down the center.

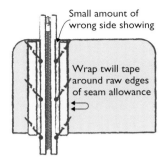

Small amount of wrong side showing

Wrap twill tape around raw edges of seam allowance

Step 19

19 Wrap the folded twill tape lengths around each of the zipper seam allowances to conceal their raw edges. If you want to space the twill tape edges just slightly away from the folded edges of the seam allowances, this will expose a small amount of the wrong side of the fabric, which provides a nice contrast. Pin the twill tape in place through all layers.

20 At each side of the zipper, topstitch the twill tape in place through all layers, with one line of stitching very close to the edge of the twill tape and one line very close to the fold of the twill tape. This should leave you with a total of four topstitched lines. Press well.

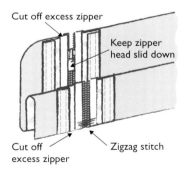

Cut off excess zipper

Keep zipper head slid down

Cut off excess zipper

Zigzag stitch

Step 21

21 Slide the zipper head back down within the edges of the Outer Flap. Carefully zigzag-stitch back and forth over the zipper teeth at the other end of the zipper, right where the edge of the Outer Flap meets the zipper. Now cut off the excess zipper length that goes beyond both edges of the Outer Flap.

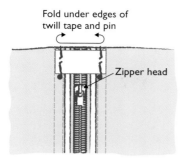

Fold under edges of
twill tape and pin

Zipper head

Step 22

22 To create a stop tab for the zipper head, lay another few inches of twill tape (unfolded) horizontally across the zipper head end of the zipper and across the folded and topstitched twill tape borders. Tuck both ends of the twill tape under so that the folds are in line with the side folds of the topstitched twill tape outer edges. Also keep the long edge of this twill tape piece in line with the edge of the Outer Flap. Keeping the open zipper teeth right next to each other, pin the twill tape in place through all layers on each side of the zipper.

23 Sew the twill tape stop tab in place with a topstitch around all four edges of the rectangle and through all layers. Be very careful as you approach the zipper teeth. To make the stitches that go over the zipper teeth, you will most likely want to switch to manually turning the machine's wheel with your hand instead of using the foot pedal so that you are less likely to break a needle. Set it aside.

24 Place the Flap Lining and Pocket Lining wrong sides together, matching their like edges. Using a ¼" seam allowance, machine-baste the layers together around all four sides. You can then treat them as one lining piece.

25 Place joined linings and the Outer Flap, right sides together. Using a ½" seam allowance, sew them together on the three sides that are joined by curved corners. (Take the same steps to be careful sewing through the zipper teeth as you did in Step 23.) Wedge-clip the curved seam allowances, turn them right side out, smooth the seams, and press well.

26 Optional: Topstitch the sewn edges of the Flap using a ⅛" seam allowance.

Assemble the Bag

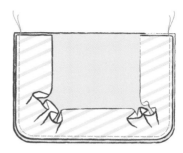

Step 27

27 With right sides together and using a ½" seam allowance, sew the Continuous Side to the Outer Front starting at the top edge of the Outer Front, around the bottom, and finishing at the top edge on the other side. Take your time around the curves to maintain an even seam allowance. (I find this step easiest when I don't use pins, and I keep the Continuous Side on top as I sew, so that I can manipulate it around the curves.) Clip the curved seam allowances, and press them toward the Continuous Side.

28 With right sides together and using a ½" seam allowance, sew the Continuous Side to the Outer Back in the same manner as Step 27. Turn right side out.

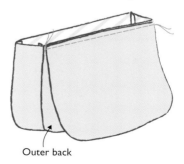

Outer back

Step 29

29 With right sides together and using a ½" seam allowance, sew the open edge of the joined Flap to the top edge of the Outer Back. (The zippered side of the Flap would be considered the right side; also be sure to center the Flap on the Outer Back between the side seams.) Press the seam allowances toward the wrong side of the Outer Back.

30 Fold the remaining top edges of the outer bag ½" toward the wrong side, and press all the way around. Set it aside.

31 Center the fusible Back Interfacing onto the wrong side of the Lining Back. Press from the fabric side lightly to fuse in place.

32 Using a chalk pencil, mark off a horizontal line on the right side of the Lining Back about 4" above the bottom edge (the bottom edge is the curved edge).

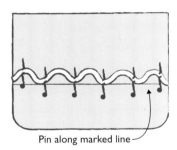

Pin along marked line

Step 33

33 Pin one end of the 1"-wide elastic to one side of the Lining Back's right side on top of the marked horizontal line. Then pin the elastic down to the Lining Back every 3½" or so across the horizontal line, and again at the opposite side of the Lining Back. Leave some slack in the elastic between the pinned points, so that the loops of elastic will be able to hold a baby bottle, water bottle for Dad, and so on. Trim off any extra length of elastic at the end.

34 Make a few lines of vertical stitching across the elastic at each of the pinned points.

35 Repeat Steps 27 and 28 with the Lining Front, Lining Back, and the Continuous Side Lining. Leave the lining wrong side out.

36 Fold the top edges of the lining ½" toward the wrong side, and press a crease all the way around.

37 Keeping the back sides against each other, fit the lining into the outer bag with wrong sides together. Align all the side seams and top edges. Begin pinning the top edges together, keeping all the side seam allowances pressed toward the sides. Keep the Flap up and its seam allowances down underneath the top folded edge of the Lining Back so that it covers the stitch line of the flap seam, and pin it in place.

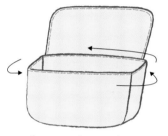

Sew around top perimeter

Step 38

38 Using a ¼" seam allowance, topstitch the top perimeter of the bag together all around. Press well around the top edges, and press the entire back well to further fuse the Back Interfacing.

Attach the Straps

39 Fold in about 1" of both ends of one of the 6" lengths of canvas strapping, and press. Then fold the length in half and press again.

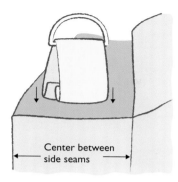

Step 40

40 Slip the pressed strapping through a D-ring, and fold the center fold down over the straight edge of the D-ring. Then sandwich the top side of the bag between the two folded edges of the strapping, so that the raw edges of the strapping are concealed against the bag. Position the folded strapping evenly between the two side seams of the bag's side, and make sure the two folded ends of the strapping are layered on top of each other evenly. Pin in place.

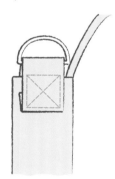

Step 41

41 Topstitch through all layers across the top, bottom, and in an "X" to simultaneously attach the strapping on the inner and outer sides of the bag securely.

42 Repeat Steps 40 and 41 on the other side of the bag.

43 With the remaining long length of strapping, fold in one end about 1" and press, loop it through the top of one of the attached D-rings, and fold it up against itself. Topstitch it to itself in the same manner as Step 41.

44 With just one side of the long strap attached, try the bag on Dad and loop the other end of the strap through the second D-ring to measure how long the strap should be. Cut at the desired length and attach the strap to itself after looping through the other D-ring in the same manner as Step 43 to finish.

Make the Changing Pad

45 Cut rectangles from the lining fabric, the outer fabric, and the quilt batting that each measure 18" × 30".

46 Lay the fabric rectangles right sides together, then lay the quilt batting rectangle against the wrong side of either of the fabric rectangles and pin them all together.

47 Using a ½" seam allowance, sew the three layers together around the perimeter, stopping about 6" from where you began. Clip off the corner seam allowances.

48 Turn right side out. Poke out the corners and smooth the seams well before pressing. Turn the open edges in ½" toward the wrong side, and press a crease.

49 Topstitch the perimeter of the pad ¼" from the edge, thereby closing the open edge of the pad in the topstitching.

50 Fold the pad in equal thirds, and press a crease on the two fold lines. Topstitch through all layers of the pad on the creased lines. Perform any further quilting stitches as desired. Tri-fold the pad and keep it in the front zipper of the Dad Bag.

-Center of Attention Quilt-

Center of Attention Quilt

*N*obody steals the spotlight like a baby, so why not quilt a stage for the new arrival? This quilt is designed for the whole family, giving each member a front-row seat for admiring. Traditional Dresden Plate stars float on a simple, square-patch background, with the center star being the largest and acting as a resting spot for baby. The number of stars that float around baby is up to you. I made one for each family member and casually scattered them to surround the center. Older siblings and family members could help choose the fabrics that will make up their own star so that it will really feel like it belongs to them. And it might not be a bad idea to let older brothers and sisters have a turn in the center every now and then, too. I don't think the little superstar will mind.

Materials

Light- to medium-weight cotton fabric:

- 6 yards for square patch background
- 1 yard for square corner accents
- 3 yards for quilt top border
- Assorted fat quarters for Dresden Plates
- 6 yards of 54–60" fabric—OR—9 yards of 44" fabric for backing
- 2 yards for bias binding

Quilt batting 120" × 120"

Quilt template plastic

Scrap of poster board or mat board

Aluminum foil

Quilting safety pins

Dresden Plate pattern pieces inside the pocket

Finished Dimensions:

Approximately 96" × 96", which is suitable for a king size bed

My Color Notes

Because I wanted the "stars" to really shine I chose bold and rich magentas, plums, golds, and some black and white in several variations of print to create the Dresden Plates. For the background squares, I chose a more muted assortment of grays, pale lavenders, and various tonal menswear checks, dots, and plaids. To add a bit of luxury, I also introduced a gray burnout velvet, which provides an interesting textural element. All of these prints and textures are framed in a graphic stripe binding that has extra charm when cut on the bias.

Trace and Cut

1 Using the quilt template plastic, trace and cut out the following Dresden Plate pattern pieces on pattern page 2: Large Blade (**A**), Small Blade (**B**), Center Circle (**C**), and Pressing Circle (**D**). Use these templates to cut the quilt pieces in Steps 2–5.

2 Cut 20 of the Large Blades (**A**) from the assorted fat quarters for the larger center Dresden Plate, being sure to transfer the "top" marking.

3 Cut 20 of the Small Blades (**B**) from the assorted fat quarters for each additional Dresden Plate, being sure to transfer the "top" marking.

4 Cut one Center Circle (**C**) from the assorted fat quarters for every Dresden Plate.

5 Cut one Pressing Circle (**D**) from the poster board.

6 Cut 49 squares from the background fabric, each measuring 13" × 13".

7 Cut 25 squares (more or less, depending on your final Dresden Plate arrangement) from the corner accent fabric, each measuring 3½" × 3½".

8 Cut two strips from the border fabric, each measuring 7" × 84".

9 Cut two strips from the border fabric, each measuring 7" × 96".

10 Cut several 4½"-wide strips on the bias from the binding fabric, so that once joined end to end, they will be approximately 11 yards in length.

Piece the Background

NOTE: Before piecing the large background squares together, you may first want to lay them out seven by seven and rearrange the configuration until you're happy with the balance of color, light, and dark.

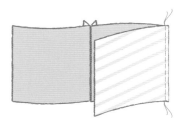

Step 11

11 With right sides together and using a ½" seam allowance, begin joining one square to another, and press the seam allowances open. Continue to join the squares side by side for a total of seven in a row.

12 Repeat Step 11 until you have seven rows comprised of seven squares in each.

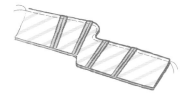

Step 13

13 With right sides together, using a ½" seam allowance and aligning seams, join a row of seven squares to another row, and press the seam allowances open.

14 Repeat Step 13 until you have joined all rows together and have a background foundation of seven by seven squares.

Piece the Dresden Plates

Step 15

15 With right sides together, fold a Large Blade in half lengthwise and sew across the top edge using a ¼" seam allowance. Repeat with 19 more Large Blades to complete enough for the larger center Dresden Plate. To save time, sew all 20 of these continuously in a chain without stopping to clip the machine threads in between, feeding another piece under the lowered machine foot as soon as the previous piece has passed through.

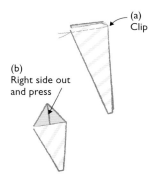

(a)
Clip

(b)
Right side out
and press

Step 16

16 (a) Snip the connecting threads between all pieces, and clip the top, folded seam allowances at an angle with each piece. (b) Turn each seam right side out to form a point, then center the seam and press from both sides.

17 With the narrow ends at the center and the pointed ends on the outer edge, arrange the twenty Large Blades right side up in a wheel configuration, and continue to rearrange them until you have a pleasing balance of color and pattern. Then stack them one on top of the other in sequence to keep them in order before they are sewn together.

Continue adding all A pieces

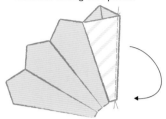

Step 18

18 With right sides together, aligning the pointed ends and with a ¼" seam allowance, sew one Large Blade piece to another. In the same manner, add another to the two that you just joined, and continue around until all 20 have been joined together. It is very important that you maintain a consistent ¼" seam allowance in this piecing, so that the circular block will lie smoothly when complete.

19 Once all 20 Large Blades have been joined side by side, join the last piece to the first to close the circle of blades. Press all seam allowances in a clockwise direction on the wrong side, and then also press well from the right side. (If the circle isn't lying quite flat, you may need to adjust the depth of some of the seam allowances.) Set them aside.

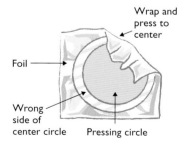

Wrap and press to center

Foil

Wrong side of center circle   Pressing circle

Step 20

20 Lay the Center Circle that you've chosen for the large center Dresden Plate right side facing down onto a slightly larger sheet of aluminum foil on the ironing board. Next, place the Pressing Circle board at the center of the wrong side of the Center Circle. Holding the Pressing Circle down in place, begin wrapping the edges of both the foil and the Center Circle in toward the center of the Pressing Circle. Smooth the foil edges into a nice crease against the edges of the Pressing Circle all around the perimeter.

21 Once the edges are smooth, press the iron directly onto the foil all around, being careful not to burn your fingers on the hot foil. Flip the circle over and press the other side at the end of the ironing board so that the bulk of the wrapped foil can extend beyond the edge of the ironing board as you press all around. Let the foil cool before removing the nicely creased Center Circle.

22 Thread and knot a hand-sewing needle. Enter the needle through the wrong side of the Center Circle and come out on the right side directly through the edge of the crease. Pull the thread slack through all the way.

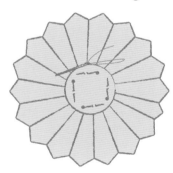

Step 23

23 Lay the Center Circle wrong side down against the center of the joined Large Blades, and pin in place. You can then begin blind-stitching (appliqué-stitching) the Center Circle to the joined Large Blades, taking care to keep your stitches hidden within the circular crease and the wrong side of the blades. Knot and clip the threads to finish. Press.

24 Repeat Steps 15–23 with additional sets of 20 Small Blades and 1 Center Circle to create as many additional Dresden Plates as you wish.

Position and Appliqué the Dresden Plates and Corner Accents

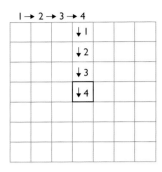

Step 25

25 Find the center square of the quilt background by counting four over from the top-left corner, and then counting four down to the center. (This step finds the center square as long as you have made the background seven by seven squares.)

26 The Large Dresden Plate should be centered over the center square so that it conceals the square entirely. Pin in place and use a blind stitch to sew the Large Dresden Plate to the quilt background. (It might be helpful to lay your work on a large table in front of you.) Press.

27 Once the Large Dresden Plate is sewn in place, find a large floor space to lay the quilt out or an open wall to pin it up before you begin placing the remaining Small Dresden Plates. (I also prefer to use quilting [curved] safety pins to attach appliqué pieces that will be sewn over a longer period of time. This prevents the pins from slipping out and you or anyone else from getting stuck while either working on the quilt or folding it up.) Continue to rearrange the Small Dresden Plates around the center Large Dresden Plate to achieve a balance of color and design that you're happy with, and then pin them all in place.

28 Sew the Small Dresden Plates to the quilt background using a blind stitch, and press. Continue until all plates are sewn in place.

Step 29

29 Press ¼" of all four sides of the Corner Accent squares back toward their wrong sides. Place the wrong side of a Corner Accent square against the right side of the quilt background at each intersection of four large squares, aligning its points with the four seams. Pin in place.

NOTE: Many of these intersections are not visible because they are covered up by the Dresden Plates, so just place them at the visible intersections.

30 Sew all Corner Accent squares in place using a blind stitch. Press.

Sew the Border, Backing, and Binding

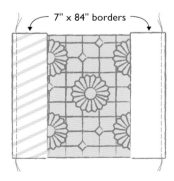

7" x 84" borders

Step 31

31 Using the 7" × 84" strips of fabric, sew each of these borders right sides together at opposite sides of the quilt top, using a ½" seam allowance. Press the seam allowances open.

32 Sew each of the 7" × 96" strips of fabric to the remaining sides of the quilt top with right sides together and using a ½" seam allowance. Press the seam allowances open.

33 Follow Steps 26–30 of the "Sixth Time's the Charm Crib Quilt" project on page 157 to assemble the batting and the backing to the quilt top.

34 After you've assembled the layers together, you can proceed with your desired quilting method, whether by hand, your machine, or a professional quilter. If you're hand-quilting, be sure to read through the "Stitch the Quilt" section on page 158 for some tips before you begin.

35 Follow Steps 31–44 of the "Quilt Binding" section on page 159 to bind the quilt.

Nest Sewing

–Nesting Cubes–

Nesting Cubes

*H*andmade toys are the best kind that you can give your own children, and they make loving gifts for expectant friends and family members. Because these are sweet and soft, they are particularly good newborn toys. Choosing colors and patterns high in contrast will help occupy even the newest baby as his eyes develop. Building, stacking, and hiding objects are all favorite skills for babies as they grow into becoming clever little toddlers. This set of Nesting Cubes helps baby begin to master those skills, and fun ribbon loops make grasping and playing easier. The sewing itself is quite simple, and you'll have some lovely handcrafted décor for your baby's nest. The more cubes you make, the higher the tower will grow, and the more giggle-y the tumbling down will be.

Materials

Light- to medium-weight woven cotton fabric:

- 10 squares of fabric measuring 8" × 8"
- 10 squares of fabric measuring 7" × 7"
- 10 squares of fabric measuring 6" × 6"
- 10 squares of fabric measuring 5" × 5"
- 10 squares of fabric measuring 4" × 4"
- 10 squares of fabric measuring 3" × 3"

Various scraps of ribbon

2 yards of heavy-duty, double-sided fusible interfacing

Spool of coordinating thread

Hand-sewing needle

Finished Dimensions:

7" square cube, 6" square cube, 5" square cube, 4" square cube, 3" square cube, 2" square cube

My Color Notes

My choices for the fabrics for these fun stacking and nesting cubes where completely determined by giving baby lots of exciting color and plenty of fussy patterns to look at while playing with the cubes.

Measure and Cut

1 Cut the fabrics of your choice, squared on the fabric's grain-line, in the measurements listed in the materials list on the left. Doing so provides enough pieces to make six cubes ranging from 2" to 7" in size. Also, keep in mind that each cube requires five squares for the outer cube and five squares for the inner cube, in case you'd like a contrasting fabric on the inside.

2 For each cube, cut five squares of heavy-duty, double-sided fusible interfacing in a measurement that is 1" shorter than the fabric squares for that cube in both directions. For instance, cut interfacing squares that are 7" × 7" for the fabric squares that are 8" × 8", and so on, until each set of fabric squares has a set of five interfacing squares.

3 Cut several 2½" lengths of ribbon for the top edge loops.

Sew the Inner and Outer Cubes

4 On the right side of the 8" square of outer fabric that you would like to be the top of the cube, mark a ½" border all around the edges with a fabric marker or fabric chalk.

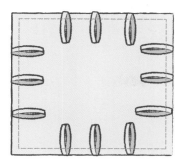

Step 5

5 Fold as many 2½" ribbon lengths as you'd like to use in half, and align their cut ends with the edge of the marked 8" square on the right side. Pin in place on each side, and then machine-baste the loops in place around the square on the marked border line. This will be the outer top of the 7" cube.

6 Center a 7" square of fusible interfacing on the wrong side of the outer top, which should fall right on the basting lines. Hold it in place as you flip the pieces over so that you can press from the right side to fuse the layers together. Set them aside.

7 With right sides together and using a ½" seam allowance, sew two of the 8" squares of outer fabric together down one side.

8 Continue to join the remaining two 8" outer squares to the two joined squares side by side in the same manner as Step 7.

Step 9

9 With right sides together and a ½" seam allowance, join the two ends of the row of four outer squares together so that you make a tube. Press all seam allowances open.

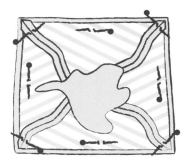

Step 10

10 Lay out the outer top piece (the one with ribbon loops) with right side facing up. With right sides together, align the bottom edge of one section of the joined outer sides to one edge of the outer top piece, and begin pinning in place all around to join the inner sides to the inner bottom. (You can make some small snips into the side edges near the side seams, no longer than about a ¼" or so, to ease fitting the sides onto the top.) Be sure the seams of the outer sides are at each of the four corners. Let the rest of the outer sides fall in a bit toward the center to keep it out of the way as you prepare to sew.

11 With a ½" seam allowance, begin sewing the outer sides to the outer top at any corner as a starting point, which should also be right in the middle of a side seam. (Your stitch line should be just to the outside of the interfacing and not through it.) As you continue around the square, stop at each corner ½" away from the edge and take a turn with your needle down. Finish this seam by overlapping the beginning of your stitches.

12 Clip the seam allowance corners of the outer cube and turn it right side out. Press the top seam allowances toward the outer sides.

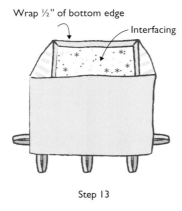

Wrap ½" of bottom edge

Interfacing

Step 13

13 One by one, place the four remaining pieces of interfacing onto the wrong sides of the outer sides, fitting them snugly up against the top edge. Wrap ½" of the bottom edge of the outer sides around the interfacing edge, and press from the right side. Continue until all sides have interfacing fused, and you have a cube formed.

NOTE: Once you are working with the smaller-size cubes, it becomes difficult to use the narrow end of the ironing board to do your pressing. So you might switch to using a rolled-up hand towel on the inside of the cube to provide some resistance as you press.

14 Repeat Steps 7–12 with five of the remaining 8" inner squares to make the inner cube. You can make your seam allowances just barely past the ½" mark as you sew, but not as deep as ⅝". This will help the inner cube fit a little better into the outer cube once the interfacing is between the two layers. Clip the seam allowance corners and trim the seam allowances around the top piece down to about ⅛". Leave the wrong side facing out.

15 Fold ½" of the bottom edge of the inner sides toward the wrong side, and press a crease around the entire bottom edge.

Assemble the Cube

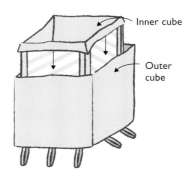

Inner cube

Outer cube

Step 16

16 With wrong sides together, place the inner cube inside the outer cube, matching the side seams, and smoothing the corners until the two cubes fit well together and their bottom edges are aligned.

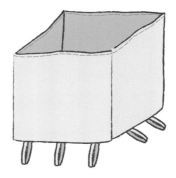

Step 17

17 Using a scant ¼" seam allowance, topstitch through all layers of the bottom edge of the cube all around the perimeter. Press well from the inner and outer cube on all sides to fuse the interfacing well.

NOTE: Once you are working with the smaller-size cubes, it becomes difficult to machine-sew the bottom edges together. You can therefore hand-sew a blind stitch at the bottom edges instead. And again, because of the small cube size, you might also switch to using a rolled-up hand towel on the inside of the cube to provide some resistance as you press.

18 Because it's difficult to reach your iron all the way up into the top corners of the cube to fuse all the layers at the corners, it's a good idea to hand-tack the corners in place. To do this, double-thread and knot a hand-sewing needle.

Then enter the needle into one of the inner top corners and come out of the top corner on the outer side. Make a few small stitches, in and out, to tack the corners together and knot the thread. Hide the thread tail between the layers, and then clip the threads close to the surface. Repeat this process with each of the remaining three corners.

19 Repeat Steps 4–18 with each set of five inner squares, five outer squares, and five interfacing squares to create various sizes of cubes for your nest.

—Henny Penny and Six Chicks—

Henny Penny and Six Chicks

Celebrating a Mama's love for her little ones, this soft hen has surprise babies hidden beneath her large, cozy wings. The chicks can Velcro on and off through plenty of stories and playtimes that you and baby will have together. Henny Penny is also shaped so that she can rock her chicks to sleep once they're all tucked in. You can make as many chicks as you wish, but six chicks fit just perfectly. She is a very patient mother.

Materials

Medium-weight woven cotton fabric (flannel works well, too)
- ½ yard for body
- ¼ yard for wings
- Various fabric scraps for chicks

12–18" of 1"-wide sew-on Velcro

Small amount of cotton quilt batting for wings

Fiberfill stuffing

Embroidery floss and needle

Henny Penny and Chicks pattern pieces inside the pocket

Finished Dimensions:
Hen: 9" × 10" × 6" **Chicks:** 2" × 2½"

My Color Notes

I thought first about how Henny Penny should feel before I thought about how she should look. So after choosing incredibly soft cotton flannels for the hen and chicks, I based the color scheme on a recognizable hen-yellow with the added fun of plum and white floral wings. Three chicks are blue tones and three chicks are pink tones in honor of my own three boys and three girls.

Trace and Cut

1   Trace and cut out the following pattern pieces from pattern pages 1 and 4: Hen Body (**A**), Hen Underside (**B**), Wing (**C**), and Chick (**D**). Be sure to trace all marks from the pattern page to the tracing paper patterns.

2   Cut one Hen Body (**A**) with the fabric folded right sides together so that you have two opposite cut pieces. Transfer the marks for the wing, Velcro strip, seam opening, and eye to both fabric pieces.

3   Cut Hen Underside (**B**) twice, and transfer the mark for the beak to the fabric piece.

4   Cut two Wings (**C**), with the fabric folded right sides together. You should have four pieces (two that are cut opposite the other two). Transfer the open seam mark.

5   Cut two Wings (**C**) from the quilt batting.

6   Cut Chick (**D**) once, with scrap fabric folded right sides together, so that you have two pieces that are cut opposite each other. Transfer the marks for the open seam to the fabric pieces. Repeat this step for as many chicks as you'd like to make.

Sew the Henny Penny

Step 7

7 Sew a 5" length of Velcro (hook side) to the Hen Body piece along the Velcro markings by topstitching along both long edges of the Velcro. Repeat on the other Hen Body.

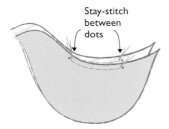

Stay-stitch between dots

Step 8

8 At the top of each Hen Body, stay-stitch between the two "leave open" dots using a ¼" seam allowance. (This helps to keep the fabric from stretching too much or becoming unraveled.)

9 At the straight edge of each of the four wing pieces, stay-stitch between the two "leave open" dots using a ¼" seam allowance.

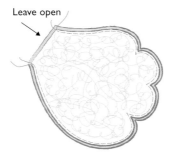

Leave open

Step 10

10 Lay two Wing fabric pieces right sides together, matching all edges, and then lay one quilt batting Wing on top of the fabric wrong side. Using a ¼" seam allowance, beginning and ending with a backstitch, sew the three layers together, taking your time around each curve and leaving the straight edge open. Clip all curved seam allowances.

11 Turn the Wing right side out and use your fingers between the inside layers to smooth all the curved edges out. Press well. Fold the edges of the open seam (including the batting) in toward the wrong side about ⅜", and press a crease.

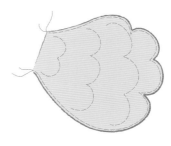

Step 12

12 Topstitch the curved edges of the Wing all around using a ½" seam allowance. You may also choose to "quilt" the Wing with some scalloped seams to emulate feather layers.

13 Attach the finished Wing to the side of the Hen Body on the wing mark by topstitching through all layers.

14 Repeat Steps 10–13 with the remaining Wing pieces and Hen Body.

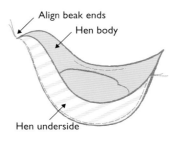

Align beak ends
Hen body
Hen underside

Step 15

15 With right sides together, aligning the beak ends of the Hen Body and the Hen Underside, and using a ¼" seam allowance, sew the Hen Underside to the bottom edge of the Hen Body. (You may choose to fold and pin the Wing to keep it out of the way of your sewing.) Clip the seam allowances.

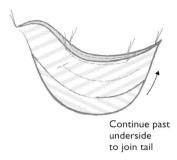

Continue past
underside
to join tail

Step 16

16 Repeat Step 7 to attach the remaining Hen Body piece to the other side of the Hen Underside piece. Start this seam at the beak end, and once you get past the Hen Underside piece, continue in the same seam to join the tail ends of the two Hen Body pieces.

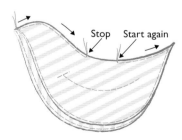

Stop   Start again

Step 17

17 Keeping the seam allowances from the last two steps, press away from the Hen Body, and starting at the beak end, sew the top edge of the two Hen Body pieces together using a ¼" seam allowance. Stop sewing once you reach the first open seam mark, and backstitch.

Begin sewing again at the next open seam mark with a backstitch, and then continue to the end of the top edge.

18 Clip off the pointed beak and tail seam allowance corners, and clip all curved seams. Carefully turn the Hen right side out, press out all the seams with your fingers, and poke out the beak and tail seams.

19 Once the Hen is smoothed out, begin stuffing it with fiberfill using only small amounts at a time, and filling the beak and tail ends first. Continue to stuff the Hen firmly, and push the bottom against a table top every now and then to ensure that it flattens out enough to stand up on its own.

20 After the Hen is sufficiently stuffed, close the open seam by hand-sewing a blind stitch, using the stay-stitch lines as a guide for seam allowances. Set Henny Penny aside.

Sew the Six Chicks

21 Stay-stitch the bottom edge of each of the Chicks between the open seam marks.

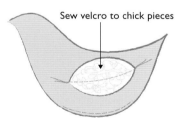

Sew velcro to chick pieces

Step 22

22 Cut the Velcro (loop side) into small wing shapes, two for each Chick. Sew a Velcro wing to each Chick on the right side using just one line of stitching through the middle of the wing.

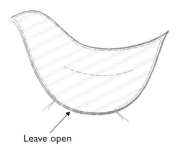

Leave open

Step 23

23 With right sides together and using a ¼" seam allowance, sew two Chick pieces together, taking your time around the points and curves. Backstitch at the beginning and end, and leave the seam open between the marks at the bottom.

24 Clip off the pointed seam allowances at the beak and tail ends, clip all other seam allowances, and turn the Chick right side out. Smooth all seams on the inside with your finger, and poke out the beak and tail.

25 Stuff the Chick with a very small amount of fiberfill, and then close the open seam by hand-sewing a blind stitch using the stay-stitch lines as a guide for seam allowances.

26 Repeat Steps 23–25 with the rest of the Chicks.

27 I recommend adding eyes by making a single French knot on each side for the Chicks and a cluster of French knots on each side for Henny Penny. (Buttons are cute for eyes, but not as safe for baby.) To make the French knot, follow these next steps.

a Hold the needle right above where the thread is emerging from the fabric, and use your opposite hand to wrap the base of the thread around the needle tip two or three times, not letting go of the thread after you've wrapped it.

b Now, still holding the thread taught, move the tip of the needle point back to the base where you first brought the needle up, and insert it right next to (but not into) the hole you came up from. As you do this, the twist of the thread on the needle should tighten as you continue to hold the thread taught with the other hand.

c Pull the thread all the way through, only leaving a little knot on the surface. Continue as many times as you wish!

-Scrappy Nap Pillow-

Scrappy Nap Pillow

*A*fter doing just a few projects in this book, you'll likely find yourself with a nice supply of colorful scraps. Or even more likely, you started with plenty of your own. Particularly after the Sixth Time's the Charm Crib Quilt, you will have some lovely scrap pieces that are perfectly suited to take a few more rounds at the cutting table and become a piece-y pillow. This is a nice-sized pillow to tuck under your arm for a little support as you sit in the nursery rocker during feeding time. Or you may be in need of a soft place to lay your head in the nursery as you spend some time getting the little one to sleep. The Scrappy Nap Pillow sews together easily, and with a removable button and a slip on-and-off design, it's just as easy to care for, too.

NOTE: Because this project has a decorative button it is not recommended that the pillow be kept in the baby's crib or sleeping place. Also children under three should only use the pillow with adult supervision.

Materials

Light- to medium-weight woven cotton fabric:
- Scraps totaling about ⅝ yard for the Pillow Front
- ½ yard for the Pillow Back

18" square pillow form

Quilt template plastic (optional)

Large button of your choice (a two-hole button is easiest to use)

Embroidery floss (or similar strong thread) and needle

Scrappy Nap Pillow pattern pieces inside the pocket

Finished Dimensions: 18" × 18"

My Color Notes

The fabrics for this pillow were repurposed from the scraps that I had left over from the Sixth Time's the Charm Quilt (see page 151). The mostly primary and secondary palette is perfect for our baby boy nursery, but not too masculine for a spirited baby girl room.

Trace and Cut

1 Using the quilt template plastic (or tracing paper), trace and cut out the following pattern from pattern page 4 Corner (**A**) and Side Center (**B**). Be sure to transfer the single notch on both pieces.

2 Cut four Corner (**A**) pieces from the fabric scraps, and mark the single notches.

3 Cut eight Side Center (**B**) pieces by folding more scraps right sides together and cutting four times. You should have four pieces facing one direction and four that are cut in the opposite direction. Mark the single notches.

4 Cut two rectangles for the Pillow back that each measure 15" × 19".

Sew the Pillow

5 With one of the pillow back rectangles, fold one of the 19" sides toward the wrong side ½", and press a crease. Fold toward the wrong side again another ½", and press a second crease. Topstitch along this double-folded edge using a ¼" seam allowance. Repeat with the other rectangle and press both well.

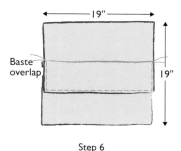

Step 6

6   Overlapping the hemmed edges from the previous step, lay the wrong side of one rectangle against the right side of the other rectangle. Keeping their side edges aligned, make the overlap deep enough so that the two pieces together create a 19" square. Pin the pieces together and baste on both sides using a ⅜" seam allowance. Set them aside.

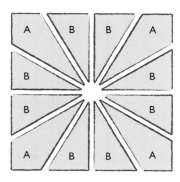

Step 7

7   To create a square, lay out the four Corner pieces in an "X" configuration and then begin to lay the Side Center pieces in among them, with all of the pieces pointing to the center. Rearrange the pieces in this configuration until you're happy with the balance of color and pattern.

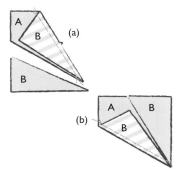

Step 8

8   Once you have a design that you like, you can group the piece into four groups. Each of the four groups will be made up of one Corner piece and the two Side Center pieces that are at either side of the Corner piece. (a) With single notches matching, right sides together, and using a ¼" seam allowance, join one of the Side Center pieces to the Corner piece. (b) Repeat with the other Side Center piece on the other side of the Corner piece. Press the seams clockwise.

9   Repeat Step 8 with the remaining groups of three pieces.

Step 10

10   Each of these joined groups will then create a square. Lay them two by two, forming a larger square so that you can double-check your desired arrangement.

11 With right sides together and using a ¼" seam allowance, sew the top two squares together. Repeat with the bottom two squares. Press the seams clockwise.

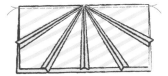

Step 12

12 Sew the joined top squares with the joined bottom squares, with right sides together and using a ¼" seam allowance. Press the seam allowance open. Press well on the right side.

13 With right sides together and using a ½" seam allowance, sew the Pillow Front to the joined Pillow Back around all four sides. Clip the corner seam allowances, and turn it right side out. Poke out the corners neatly.

14 Insert the pillow form through the overlapped back sides, and smooth the rectangles back in place over each other.

15 Double-thread a very long length of embroidery floss through the needle. Find the center of the Pillow Back by crossing a string or thread from opposite corners twice, and marking where they overlap.

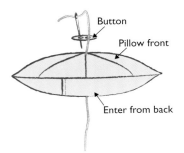

Button
Pillow front
Enter from back

Step 16

16 Enter the needle through the center of the Pillow Back, and press the pillow down from the front so that the needle can exit through the front, just to the side of the center seam intersection, and pull through, but not all

the way. Then enter the needle through the back side of one of the button's holes. Insert the needle back down through the button in the other hole, and then insert the needle just to the other side of the center intersection. Poke the needle through to the back right next to where you began, and pull through the slack, but be sure to keep the tail from slipping through.

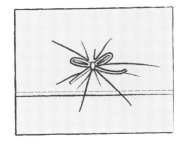

Step 17

17 Holding both ends of the thread, clip the threads to remove the needle end. Now tie the double threads together in a knot, and tighten the knot as you do so to draw the button into the center tightly. Knot a few times to secure it. Clip the excess thread length.

18 Repeat Steps 16 and 17 each time you need to remove the pillow cover for laundering.

—Daydreams Mobile and Lampshade—

Daydreams Mobile and Lampshade

*I*f you've ever let out a sad sigh as you packed up nursery items that didn't quite grow with your baby into their big kid room, this is the project for you. Using a plain lampshade as a starting point, this design first serves as a charming mobile to hang above the crib. Then, as obvious as this may seem, the mobile can grow up and be the lampshade it was always meant to be. The flora and fauna are simply fused onto the lampshade using an iron, and they have sweet, hand-stitched details to look as though they've been sewn to the shade. The dangling charms are made from the same templates, and can be assembled with hand-stitching or on the sewing machine before they are dangled from the shade's rim.

Materials

Various solid and printed fabric scraps for silhouette shapes

A few 9" × 12" sheets of Steam-A-Seam fusible interfacing

A plain, smooth-surfaced lampshade in a light color (preferably one that has three metal support bars at the top)

Fiberfill, a small amount

Embroidery floss and needle

Embroidery hoop (optional)

Buttons or any other desired trims

Craft string for hanging

Screw-eye for anchoring in the ceiling

Daydreams Mobile and Lampshade pattern pieces inside the pocket

---

Finished Dimensions:
The finished size is dependant on the size lampshade used.

My Color Notes

The mobile silhouettes are made up of mostly lavenders, blues, and greens which really pop against Roman's yellow nursery walls. I kept all the prints very small so they are "readable" within the small silhouettes. And I also chose prints that had some pretty floral elements that were easy to cut out and use as additional shapes in the mobile's composition.

Trace and Cut

1   Trace and cut out each of the various sizes of birds, wings, leaves, and branches on page 137.

2   For the silhouettes that you will fuse to the lampshade, use the paper patterns and a fabric marker to draw the silhouettes onto the right sides of the various scraps of fabric. You may choose to flip the patterns over on the opposite side to trace, so that you can also make birds that are facing opposite directions.

Stitch and Compose the Shapes

Step 3

3   Using colorful embroidery floss and an embroidery needle, follow the traced lines of the silhouette with a running stitch all the way around. (If your scraps are big enough and you'd like the help of an embroidery hoop, have at it.)

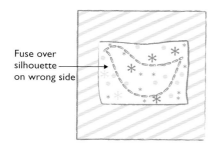

Fuse over silhouette on wrong side

Step 4

4 From the wrong side of the fabric, you can see the outlines of the silhouette because of the running stitches. Cut a piece of Steam-A-Seam a bit larger than the silhouette shape. Using the iron, fuse one side of the Steam-A-Seam to the wrong side of the fabric over the silhouette shape. (To fuse only one side, leave one of the two backing papers on the Steam-A-Seam sheet, place the sticky side down against the wrong side of the fabric, and then press.)

5 After you have fused the Steam-A-Seam in place, cut the silhouette out, leaving a fabric border of just about ¼" all around the silhouette. Leave the remaining paper backing on for the time being.

6 Repeat Steps 2–5 for as many silhouettes from various fabrics as you wish until you have plenty to play around with.

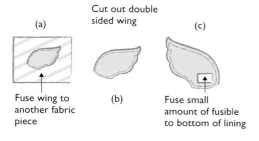

Cut out double sided wing

(a)

Fuse wing to another fabric piece

(b)

(c)

Fuse small amount of fusible to bottom of lining

Step 7

7 Following Steps 2–5 for the wing silhouettes will create flat wings for the birds. If you'd like some wings to flap out a bit, continue with the following after Steps 2–5: (a) fuse the wing (one that has already been stitched, fused, and cut out) to the wrong side of another piece of fabric. (b) Then cut the shape of the wing out once more using the first wing as your template. (c) Fuse another piece of Steam-A-Seam to just the bottom portion of the wing (either fabric side), leaving one of the backing papers on.

8 Begin to compose your scene on the surface of the lampshade by peeling off the paper backings from the silhouettes and lightly laying, and gently sticking, the fusible side of the silhouettes to the lampshade. The pieces will continue to be removable so that you can rearrange the elements until you like what you see. Overlap the wing silhouettes on top of the bird silhouettes.

9 Once you have all the elements in place to your liking, begin to fuse the silhouettes to the shade, pressing with the iron on the outside while you use a rolled-up towel in your hand from the inside to provide some resistance behind each piece. The flapping wings can be pressed into place on the bird's side, and then just let the top portions fold out from the shade. Continue until all pieces are fused.

Create the Dangling Elements

10 Fold some fabric wrong sides together and trace the bird silhouette onto one of the right sides. Pin the two layers together in the center of the silhouette, and outside of it as well.

11 With the embroidery floss, begin a running stitch through both layers, wrong sides together and following the traced lines of the silhouette. Stop stitching when you are about an inch or two away from where you started. (You may want these stitches to be a bit smaller than the fused silhouettes, as they will be functional and hold a bit of stuffing in between two layers of fabric.)

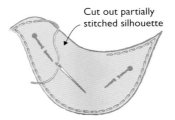

Cut out partially stitched silhouette

Step 12

12 Gather the threaded needle out of the way as you cut the silhouette out of the fabric, leaving a fabric border of about ¼" all the way around the traced lines and stitch lines.

13 Using very tiny amounts of fiberfill at a time, begin to stuff a very small amount in between the two layers of fabric through the opening left by your unfinished stitching. Poke the stuffing gently into each corner to fill the shape out.

14 Once you have the amount of stuffing dimension that you like for the silhouette, continue the running stitch to close the edge seam, and then knot to finish.

15 For the dangling bird wings, follow Steps 10 and 11, but finish the running stitch without using any fiberfill in the wings. You can then hand-stitch a double-sided wing on each side of the stuffed bird by sewing back and forth through the bird to attach the wings. (You may also choose to add some tiny buttons for the bird's eyes.)

16 Repeat Steps 10–15 with as many dangling silhouettes as you'd like for the lampshade.

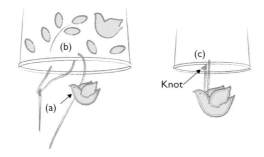

Step 17

17 Use a long length of colorful embroidery floss and a sharp needle to begin attaching the dangling silhouettes

from the bottom edge of the lampshade. (a) Begin by poking the threaded needle (don't knot the thread at the end) through the top of the silhouette's seam allowance, leaving plenty of slack, (b) then poke the needle into the outer side of the lampshade just above the rim and pull it through the inside of the shade a bit. Take the needle off the thread. Decide how high or low you'd like the silhouette to hang by pulling the thread up and down. (c) Tie the loose ends of the thread into a knot at your desired height, clip off the excess thread, and slide the thread through the silhouette and the shade until the knot is hidden at the inner edge of the shade.

18 Repeat Step 17 to attach all the dangling silhouettes.

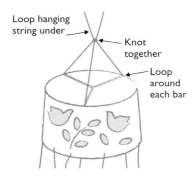

Loop hanging string under

Knot together

Loop around each bar

Step 19

19 To hang it from the ceiling, use equal lengths of craft string looped and tied around each of the three support bars at the top of the lampshade. Hold all three together in your hand and let the shade hang down. Make sure you hold the shade level, and then knot all strands together in one slip knot. Loop a longer length of string underneath this knot, and use this to hang from a screw-eye in the ceiling. You need to consider the weight of your finished mobile and the type of ceiling that you have to determine the safest way to hang the piece. You may find that you should use a drywall anchor or a similar support with the screw-eye.

20 To use as a lampshade, remove all hanging strings from the top support bars, and attach to a lamp with lamp finial.

bird wing

bird body

bird wing

bird body

leaf

leaf

leaf

branch

leaf

—Writing on the Walls—

Writing on the Walls

There are all sorts of ways to personalize your baby's nursery, but nothing could be more personal than handmade words. Should your new one be sharing a room with an older sibling, this is a nice way to designate a special baby space. You can spell out baby's name, initials, birth date, or a wishful word such as "rest." The project is based mostly on embroidery and appliqué work, and I recommend pulling in both printed and solid fabrics to help create the nostalgic feel of these little artworks. My final pieces are stretched across canvases that vary in size and shape, creating a lyrical look, which is further helped along by hanging them at different heights. You can also take all the same techniques taught in this project and apply them to pillow fronts, quilt blocks, or any other heirloom item for your little one.

Materials

Various light- to medium-weight woven cottons (muslin works great for this project):

- For the backgrounds, you'll need squares or rectangles that are about 8" larger in both directions than your desired finished size for each canvas (for example, 20" × 20" fabric for a 12" × 12" canvas).
- For the letters that are appliquéd, you'll need pieces of fabric that are an inch or so larger in both directions than your letter size.
- For the letters that are both embroidered and appliquéd, you'll need pieces of fabric that are as large as the backgrounds (this is so you can fit them into an embroidery hoop before you cut out the letter).

Small amount of lightweight fusible interfacing (one-sided) for the appliquéd letters

Spool of coordinating thread for appliqué

Appliqué needle

Assorted colors of embroidery floss like DMC Perle Cottons

Embroidery needle

Embroidery hoop, ideally larger than your letters

Computer printer and plain paper for tracing a specific font style

Pre-stretched canvas for each letter in desired size and shape

Staple gun and staples

Finished Dimensions:

Dimensions will vary depending on the size canvases you choose for each letter.

My Color Notes

I kept the tones for my "BABY" canvases soft by combining cream-colored muslin with fresh and sometimes acidic greens, blues, and yellows. By keeping the color family harmonious, the details of texture and stitch work can be accentuated even more. Each canvas does carry a small pop of orange, either in the print or in the stitching, for added interest and playfulness.

Compose the Word

1   Once you've decided on both the word and the size of each letter, use your computer to print out one letter per 8½" × 11" page. Save ink by printing the letter color in grayscale, but ideally it should be dark enough to see through fabric for tracing. If your fabric is printed or dark in color, you can also cut the letter out from the paper and then use it as a tracing template on top of the fabric.

NOTE: The following instructions detail three different methods of making these letter canvases, so feel free to use all the methods for a variation, or just choose one method if you like.

Method 1: Embroidered Letters on a Single Background

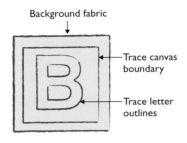

Step 2

2   Trace the letter onto the background fabric using a water-soluble fabric marker (or a light fabric-chalk pencil if the fabric is dark in color). You might first try taping the letter onto a window during daylight hours, and then taping the fabric on top for tracing. In addition to tracing the letter outlines, trace in any other designs that you would like for the piece to have, either inside or outside the letter or both. You might try referencing embroidery books, or any other design books and fabrics that have small elements that you can trace onto the fabric for inspiration. Keep in mind the shape and size of the canvas you'll use as you design the piece. You might want to sketch in the canvas size around your letter with the water-soluble marker as well, so that you keep all your handiwork within the canvas borders.

3   Once you are finished tracing, stretch the fabric onto an embroidery hoop and tighten until the fabric is relatively taut in all directions but slack enough that you aren't skewing the letter or design work one way or another.

4   For the capital "B," I began by making an outline of the B using a chain stitch. To begin the chain stitch, thread and knot your embroidery floss (I used all six strands), and then bring the needle up from underneath, out the top, and pull the slack all the way through.

Step 5

5   Hold down the thread a tiny amount next to where it just came out using the opposite hand you sew with. Insert the needle back into the hole it came up through, continuing to hold the thread down as you pull through so that the entire stitch doesn't slip back through.

Step 6

6   While there is still a loop left on top, poke the needle back up a stitch length away from where you started, pass the needle through the loop to catch it, and pull the slack all the way through.

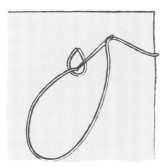

Step 7

7   Insert the needle down right next to where you just came out of and then back down through the top a stitch distance away. Poke the needle through your slack again as you pull through to catch the next loop. Continue along the traced lines with this stitch until you reach the end.

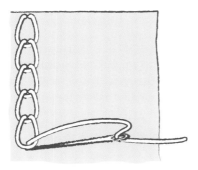

Step 8

8   At the end, insert the needle straight down on the other side of the last loop you've made to anchor it. Knot underneath, weave back through some of the underneath stitching, and trim the threads.

9   The design inside the capital "B" is just very simple concentric rows of running stitches in a second color. Make these inside the letter, just following the direction of the letter itself. If you want some help keeping your lines straight, you could use a ruler to draw some guidelines along the straight passes of the letter.

Step 10

10   For the stitch design outside the letter, I chose to make more sparse designs so that they wouldn't compete with the letter. So you might try embroidery floss that is lighter in color than the letter, and also stitches that aren't too close together. To create the glittering star designs that I made, begin by stitching an asterisk with four long stitches that cross each other in the center. Then anchor the asterisk in the center by crossing over with two small stitches that wrap around the intersection.

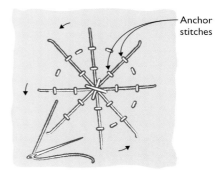

Anchor stitches

Step 11

11   With a second, lighter color, you can continue to anchor each bar of the asterisk down with tiny stitches starting right next to the center intersection. This is done most easily by going in a circular fashion around the asterisk from one bar to the next, each stitch an equal distance from the intersection until all eight bars have been anchored. Then move a little farther away from the center and continue another row of anchors that circle around the bars, and also make a few "sparkle" stitches in between the bars if you wish.

12 To carry out the sparkles farther, simply continue to let tiny stitches surface as the concentric rows of stitching around the asterisk spread larger and larger.

Method 2: Printed Appliqués on a Printed Background

13 For the letter and the background, choose two prints of fabric that you like together, keeping in mind that you want one to show up well against the other.

14 Cut out the letter template from the paper, making sure your cut lines are nice and smooth.

15 Trace the letter onto the fusible side of the interfacing. Cut out the interfacing letter.

16 Press to fuse the interfacing letter onto the wrong side of the fabric you'd like to use for the printed letter.

17 Once the interfacing is pressed well, cut the fabric around the letter, leaving a fabric border of about ½" all around the edges of the interfacing letter. Then clip the fabric border around the letter close to the interfacing's edge, but not all the way, stopping about ⅛" from the edge.

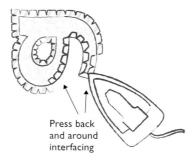

Press back
and around
interfacing

Step 18

18 To make smooth folded edges on the letter, wrap the wrong side of the fabric borders around the interfacing letter and press. This will take a little nit-picky time to get right, and inner corners can be a challenge to turn in smoothly, so take your time and clip further where necessary. It can also be helpful to use an awl or a long straight pin to hold the fabric fold over in place with one hand while you press with the other.

Step 19

19 Place the wrong side of the letter against the right side of the printed background fabric and position as desired. Make some large basting stitches by hand through the letter and the background to hold the letter in place.

20 To secure the letter to the background, appliqué-stitch the letter's folded edges to the background (with regular sewing thread). The appliqué stitch is similar to a blind stitch. As you sew, you'll likely need to continue to fold the edges of the letter underneath to reestablish the smooth folded edge. Using the point of your needle to nudge the fabric under right before you stitch it down is known as needle-turn appliqué. (It should be noted that if you're not comfortable with this technique, there is no harm in using a visible running stitch or whipstitch around the letter's edges to secure it to the background.)

21 To add just a little more interest, stretch the background fabric into the embroidery hoop and make a running stitch into the background with the embroidery floss right up against all edges of the letter. You may also choose to make more stitches on the printed background to outline various elements of the design.

Method 3: Embroidered and Appliquéd Letters

Step 22

22 Begin by tracing your letter onto a solid, light-colored fabric or muslin. Trace some floral elements within the inside of the letter as well.

23 Also trace the letter onto the fusible side of the interfacing, but make your tracing slightly larger than the letter around all edges by about ⅛". Set the interfacing letter aside.

24 Stretch the fabric with the tracing onto the embroidery hoop and tighten. Make a chain stitch to outline the letter, as detailed in Steps 4–8.

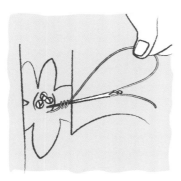

Step 25

25 For the flower centers, make five or six French Knots nestled next to each other. (I used all six strands of the embroidery floss for this.) To make a French Knot, hold

the thread right above where it is emerging from the fabric, and use your opposite hand to wrap the base of the thread around the needle tip two or three times.

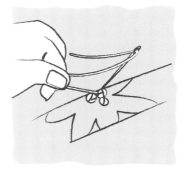

Step 26

26 Still holding the thread, move the tip of the needle point back to the base where you first brought the needle up, and insert it right next to (but not into) the hole you came up from. As you do this, the twist of thread on the needle should tighten as you continue to hold the thread taut with the other hand.

27 Pull the thread all the way through, leaving only a little knot on the surface.

Step 28

28 For each flower petal, make satin stitches using only three strands of the embroidery floss. A satin stitch is made just like you would think: simple stitches from one side to the other and packed right up against each other. The satin stitch should look the same on the back side of your work as it does on the front side. Just be sure that you enter the needle right into your traced lines on each side to keep the edges smooth and consistent.

29 Once all the flower petals are complete, fill in the remaining space inside the letter with more French Knots.

30 When all the embroidery inside the letter is complete, press the interfacing letter to the wrong side of the embroidered letter, making sure all the edges are matched up.

31 Follow Step 17 to cut out the letter.

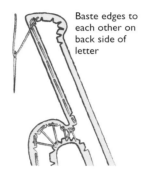

Baste edges to each other on back side of letter

Step 32

32 Instead of pressing the edges of fabric around the interfacing letter, just turn them back and press a crease with your fingers. Then make some simple basting stitches on the back to keep the fabric edges turned against the interfacing and in place before you sew the letter to the fabric background.

33 Position the embroidered letter in place on the fabric background and secure it by following Steps 19 and 20.

Mount to the Canvas

34 Before you stretch the pieces to the canvases, press them well. Do not press down hard on the heavily embroidered areas, because you want to let details such as French Knots stay nice and fluffy. But do press the main fabric areas well.

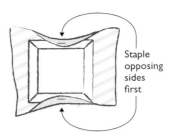

Staple opposing sides first

Step 35

35 Lay your piece down, wrong side facing up, and then center the right side of the canvas against it. Pull one edge of the fabric piece around to the back edge of the canvas and staple it in the center. Then repeat at the opposite side of the fabric piece, this time giving it a little tug to stretch it just a bit before stapling.

36 Repeat the subtle stretching and stapling at the center of the remaining two sides of the fabric piece. Flip it over to make sure the letter is in your desired position.

37 If the canvas is round or oval, continue to stretch and staple all the way around, keeping your staples about an inch apart.

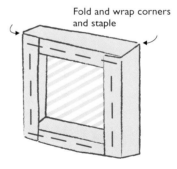

Fold and wrap corners and staple

Step 38

38 If the canvas is square or rectangular, continue to stretch and staple the fabric piece to the back on each side until you are about 2" from the corners. Turn and fold each corner in toward the back neatly so that the canvas sides are smooth, and then finish stapling to secure the corners.

39 Hang the canvases on nails at your desired height. You can use a blow dryer on a low setting to gently dust them as needed.

-Hide and Seek
Spectrum Quilt-

Hide and Seek Spectrum Quilt

With each new baby in our family, we have always had a new "play quilt." Our play quilts get dragged from one room to another so that baby always has a soft, clean place to roll around and discover toes, fingers, and other wonders. While we typically place a toy here and there around the quilt with baby, I thought it would be fun if the quilt was a bit of a toy in itself. This one has little printed surprises hiding behind a fabric door on each colorful block. Choose hiding prints to coordinate with each of the solid color blocks and then use this quilt as a color teaching tool as baby grows into more discoveries. Maybe you'd like your little one to discover fun images such as frogs or puppies behind the doors. There are endless printed options to choose from at your local fabric shop, so think of a theme that you'd like to share with your curious child. This quilt can even serve as fun playroom wall décor long after your baby has grown out of rolling around on it (but who really outgrows that?).

Materials

Light- to medium-weight quilting cottons:

- Two versions of nine different solid colors (light and dark). A fat quarter (a quarter yard cut by cutting one yard into a quadrant instead of 9" strips) of each of the 18 colors
- Nine 6½" squares of printed fabric

2½ yards of 60" cotton muslin (or cream/white-colored fabric) for sashing and backing

60" × 60" of cotton quilt batting

Spool of 100-percent cotton coordinating thread for machine piecing

Spool each of nine colors of perle cotton thread for hand quilting

Hand-quilting needle (or embroidery needle if your quilting thread is particularly thick)

Finished Dimensions: 48" × 48"

My Color Notes

When making the full spectrum of colors shown with this quilt, it's a good idea to have a color wheel on hand. It might be easiest to start by finding the two solid tones of eight colors that surround the center black/gray block. Then the fun of picking the prints to hide under each solid door is made much easier.

Measure and Cut

NOTE: The following cutting is easiest when you have the help of a clear quilting ruler, rotary cutter, and cutting mat.

1   From the lighter shades of each of the nine solid colors, cut the following pieces:

- two squares measuring 6½" × 6½"
- two rectangles measuring 10½" × 1½"
- two rectangles measuring 12½" × 1½"

2 From the darker shades of each of the nine solid colors, cut the following pieces:

- two rectangles measuring 2½" × 6½"
- two rectangles measuring 2½" × 10½"

3 Cut one 6½" square from each of the nine printed fabrics. Group all the cut fabrics by color in nine sets.

4 From the muslin, cut the following pieces:

- two rectangles that are 6½" × 36½"
- two rectangles that are 6½" × 48½"

Piece a Block

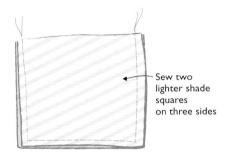

Sew two lighter shade squares on three sides

Step 5

5 With right sides together and using a ¼" seam allowance, sew three sides of the two lighter-shade 6½" squares together in one continuous U-shaped seam. Clip the corners, turn right side out, and press well. This is one of the fabric "doors."

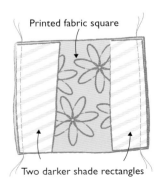

Printed fabric square

Two darker shade rectangles

Step 6

6 With right sides together and using a ¼" seam allowance, sew one of the darker-shade 2½" × 6½" rectangles to one side of the printed 6½" square. Repeat with the remaining similar rectangle on the opposite side of the 6½" square. Press the seam allowances out, away from the center.

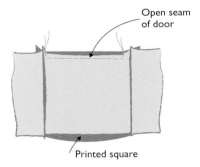

Open seam of door

Printed square

Step 7

7 Center the door over the right side of the printed square between the two seams from Step 6. Align the open edges of the door with one of the two remaining unsewn sides of the printed square. Machine-baste the door in place using a ¼" seam allowance.

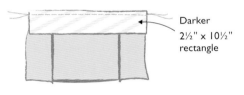

Darker 2½" x 10½" rectangle

Step 8

8 On the same side that you basted in Step 7, lay one of the darker-shade 2½" × 10½" rectangles with right sides together, and align the edges of the rectangle with the joined printed square, side rectangles, and door. Sew them together using a ¼" seam allowance. Press the piece and seam allowances out, away from the center.

9 Flip the door open to keep it out of the way, and using a ¼" seam allowance, sew the remaining darker-shade 2½" × 10½" rectangle to the other side of the joined printed square and smaller side rectangles. Press the piece and seam allowances out, away from the center.

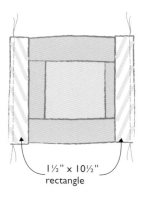

1½" × 10½" rectangle

Step 10

10 With right sides together and using a ¼" seam allowance, sew each of the 1½" × 10½" rectangles on opposite sides of the joined pieces, layering them onto the edges that have seam intersections from previous steps. Press all seam allowances out, away from the center.

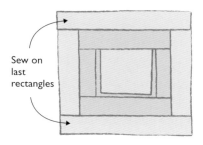

Sew on last rectangles

Step 11

11 With right sides together and using a ¼" seam allowance, sew each of the remaining 1½" × 12½" rectangles onto the other two edges of the darker-shade rectangles. Press the seam allowances out, away from the center. The finished block should look like the figure above.

12 Repeat Steps 5–11 with each of the eight remaining sets of color block pieces.

Assemble the Blocks

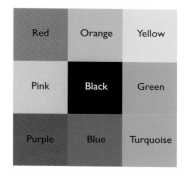

Red	Orange	Yellow
Pink	Black	Green
Purple	Blue	Turquoise

Step 13

13 Once all of the blocks are complete, arrange them in your desired 3" × 3" configuration. For balance, I chose to place the black block at the center and then let the spectrum flow around it in rainbow order, as shown in the figure above. You may also want to make sure that all the doors are opening in the same direction, so that if you'd like to eventually hang the quilt on a playroom wall, there won't be any doors flapping open.

14 With right sides together and using a ¼" seam allowance, join the top three blocks together side by side, and press the seam allowances open.

15 Repeat Step 14 with the center row of three blocks and the bottom row of three blocks.

16 In one continuous seam, with right sides together and using a ¼" seam allowance, sew the top row of three blocks to the center row of three blocks (making sure you are joining the correct sides based on your desired color flow). Press the seam allowance open.

17 Repeat Step 16 to attach the bottom row of three blocks to the other side of the center row of three blocks.

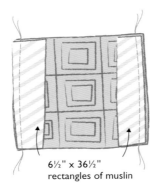

6½" × 36½"
rectangles of muslin

Step 18

18 If some inconsistencies have occurred in your piecing of the blocks, causing the size of the joined blocks to be either larger or smaller than 36½" × 36½", you'll want to adjust the size of the cream-colored sashing accordingly. With right sides together and using a ¼" seam allowance, sew each of the two 6½" × 36½" cream-colored rectangles to opposite sides of the joined quilt blocks (it doesn't matter which two sides). Press the seams open.

19 Sew each of the remaining two cream-colored 6½" × 48½" rectangles to the remaining two sides of the joined blocks with right sides together and using a ¼" seam allowance. Press the seams open.

20 The layers of this quilt come together more like a pillow than a typical quilt with binding. Once all the seams on the quilt top have been pressed well, cut a layer of batting and a layer of backing fabric to the same size as the finished quilt top.

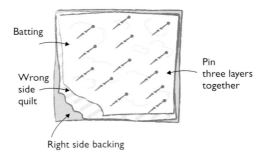

Batting

Wrong side quilt

Pin three layers together

Right side backing

Step 21

21 To assemble the layers, lay the quilt top and the backing right sides together. Next, layer the batting on top of the quilt top's wrong side. Pin the three layers together in several places—at least at all block corners, and a few in the sashing—with either quilting straight pins or safety pins.

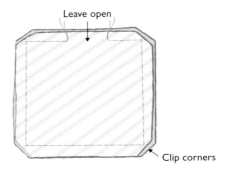

Leave open

Clip corners

Step 22

22 Using a ½" seam allowance, sew around all four sides of the three layers, but stop sewing about 10" from where you began, so that there is an opening in one side. Clip off the corner seam allowances and remove the pins holding the layers together.

23 Flip the quilt right side out, and smooth out the seams and corners from the inside using your fingers. Turn the edges of the opening in toward each other by ½", and press a crease on the backing and the quilt top. Pin this opening closed and blind-stitch it shut.

24 After you've pressed the quilt well from both sides, pin the layers together again in several places. Using a ½" seam allowance from the quilt edge, topstitch all four sides of the quilt with cream-colored thread.

25 Keeping the pins in and starting at the center, hand-quilt the layers together however you like. I quilted around each of the block "doors" with coordinating perle cotton thread. I also drew some guideline dashes with a water-soluble pen around the sashing to make several rows of multi-colored stitching about ½" apart from each other. By doing both, the reverse side of the quilt will have beautiful little rows and squares of rainbow stitches. For more in-depth advice on hand-quilting, see page 158.

Sixth Time's the Charm Crib Quilt

Sixth Time's the Charm Crib Quilt

*W*hether baby is the first or the tenth, you can celebrate their arrival by making this charming quilt. This more-simple-than-it-looks design was inspired by our own little number six, and the new angle he's brought to our family—the hexagon. What starts out as colorful strips of various lengths and widths will eventually be joined into rectangles, then cut and composed into a hexagon, and finally trimmed to the rectangular crib shape. The bonus of this quilt is that the process will leave you with plenty of pieced-together scraps ready to be made into other patchwork nursery accessories. And, of course, you'll have a beautiful quilt. Oh, and a cozy baby, too!

Materials

Various colors and/or prints of light- to medium-weight cotton fabrics for quilt top

2 yards lightweight cotton for backing

1 yard lightweight cotton for binding

Cotton quilt batting (at least 40" × 60")

Quilting ruler (6" × 24" clear with grid is a great option)

Quilting 60-degree Equilateral Triangle Ruler

Rotary cutter and mat

Yardstick

Spool or two of neutral 100-percent cotton thread

Masking tape

Quilting safety pins (curved are great)

Large hand-basting needle

Quilting frame or hoop (optional)

Hand-quilting thread in desired colors

Hand-quilting needle or embroidery needle

Finished Dimensions: Approximately 38" × 54"

My Color Notes

Sometimes choosing a specific palette for me has more to do with specifically omitting colors than it does with specifically including colors. For this quilt I wanted mostly blues, whites, yellows, and browns with shots of green, red, and orange. I very specifically did not want any pinks, purples, or magentas. So the result is boyish and well grounded.

Arrange Your Fabrics

Before cutting, I chose to first arrange my quilt-top fabric in general color groups. For instance, I placed all the reds and oranges together, greens and blues together, yellows and browns together, and so on. You may prefer to arrange them in piles of light, medium, and dark. Doing either of these arrangement styles now, will give you a little more control as you begin composing the rows of strips together.

Cut Fabrics and Join Strips

If you have your fabrics arranged by color, after you begin cutting, continue to group like-colored and like-size strips into their own piles. For example, you'll have piles of 1½"-wide reds and oranges, 2"-wide reds and oranges, 3"-wide reds and oranges, and so on. Then you'll have similar width-related piles for all the other color categories.

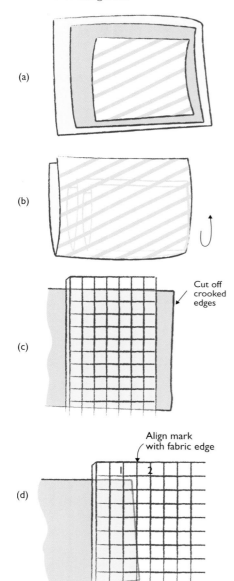

(a)

(b)

(c)

Cut off crooked edges

(d)

Align mark with fabric edge

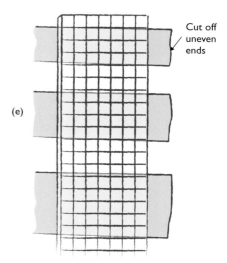

(e)

Cut off uneven ends

NOTE: You can save time by: (a) layering several fabrics on top of one another, and by (b) folding them over one or more times to make cuts. (c) First trim off any crooked edges. (d) Then, using your clear, rectangular quilt ruler, begin cutting your fabrics into strips of various lengths and widths. (e) Cut the ends of the strips so that they are square.

1   Using the suggestions with the figure sequence on this page, and with a quilt ruler, rotary cutter, and mat, begin cutting your fabrics into 1½"-, 2"-, 3"-, and 4"-wide strips. Be sure to cut the strips straight on the fabric grain or crossgrain.

2   Group together all of your 1½"-wide strips, but also order them from one color category to the next. In other words, the top of your pile will be a whole section of reds, then a whole section of yellows, and so on, but all in the same 1½" pile.

Step 3

3 With right sides together and using a ½" seam allowance, join all the 1½"-wide strips, end to end in color sequence, to create one (very long) continuous 1½"-wide pieced strip. Begin and end each seam with a backstitch. To save time, try the loop chain method above. This way, you don't have to cut your machine threads every time you join a strip. You would simply pull the strip and threads away from the machine a few inches, then take the opposite end of the strip you just joined and sew the next strip to it.

4 Once you've joined all the 1½"-wide strips, clip the machine threads in between each joining, to release them from the looping method. Press all the seams open.

5 Cut the one continuous 1½" strip into several 60" lengths. Set any leftover material that isn't 60" long aside.

6 Repeat Steps 3–5 with the 2"-wide strips, then with the 3"-wide strips, and finally with the 4"-wide strips.

Assemble the Rows

7 You can now regroup all 60" lengths into color categories again, regardless of their width. While you may have a given 60" strip that has more than one color category in it, this will only contribute to the fun randomness of the quilt design.

8 You can now begin to compose a rectangle with these strips, by laying one row above another. Just randomly choose widths and colors in this process until you like what you see, and also until you've lined up enough rows to add up to 36–40" in height.

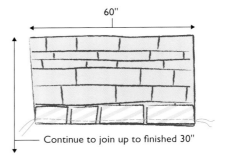

60"

Continue to join up to finished 30"

Step 9

9 With right sides together and using a ¼" seam allowance, begin sewing the strips together on their long sides in your desired order from Step 8.

10 Press all the seam allowances in one direction on the wrong side, and press on the right side as well. Double-check your finished rectangle to be sure that it is at least 30" × 60". If it is not quite 30", sew enough strips to make it at least this size. If it is more than 30", trim it down to size.

Cut Triangles

NOTE: Simply put, if you have a large-scale rotary mat that has grid markings as well as several angle markings on it, you can use the 60-degree angle marking, and a yardstick to make the triangular cuts into your rectangles. But do follow through the steps below for more specifics.

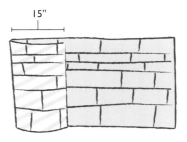

15"

Step 11

11 Lay the rectangle right side up on your cutting mat. Fold the rectangle from the left to the right until the overlap is 15" wide, and keep the top and bottom edges in line neatly.

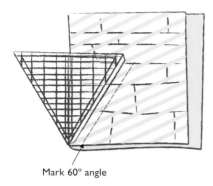

Mark 60° angle

Step 12

12 Lay the 60-degree triangular ruler, with the center point at the very bottom edge, over the rectangle's fold so that the fold itself is passing through the center line of the triangle. By doing so, half the ruler should be on the cutting mat and half should be on the folded fabric. Keeping the triangular ruler in place, make a few marks on the fabric just to the right with fabric chalk to mark the angle of the triangle.

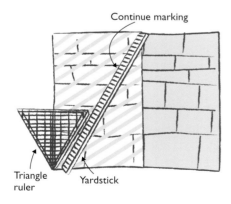

Continue marking

Triangle ruler   Yardstick

Step 13

13 Holding the triangle firmly in place, lay a yardstick right up against the right edge of the triangle so that you are continuing the 60-degree angle farther up the rectangle. Hold the yardstick firmly in place, and continue marking the angle all the way up the rectangle with fabric chalk.

14 Cut on these marks after removing the triangular ruler, and placing the yardstick on either side of the marks that is most comfortable for you to cut. After unfolding the cut triangle, you should be left with a 60-degree triangle that is 30" tall.

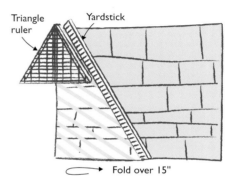

Triangle ruler   Yardstick

Fold over 15"

Step 15

15 After setting aside the loose scrap and the 60" right triangle from the cut you made in Step 14, take the bottom-left point of the larger remaining piece and fold it from left to right again, until the overlap at the bottom edge is 15". The cut edge from the previous step will help you establish your next cut line, but use your triangular ruler and yardstick again to check all the lines, and help stabilize your cut. Cut along the 60-degree line again to make a second 30"-tall triangle. Set aside the excess scrap from the cut.

16 Repeat Steps 8–15 to create another 30" × 60" rectangle, and cut two more 60-degree triangles from it, so that you have four triangles that are 30" tall.

17 Repeat Steps 8–15 again; however, amend the dimensions of the rectangle (and therefore triangles) to be only 27" × 60".

NOTE: You should now have four triangles that are 30" tall, and two triangles that are 27" tall.

Assemble the Triangles

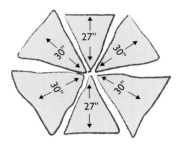

Step 18

18 Lay out your triangles into a pie shape with the two 27"-tall triangles in the center top and bottom positions, and the four 30" triangles to the left and right of the top and bottom triangles, as shown in the figure above. Rearrange the triangles until you have your desired balance of color and design. (Keep in mind that the 27" triangles can switch places with each other, and the 30" triangles can switch places with each other, but the layout of triangle sizes cannot change from what is shown in the figure above.)

NOTE: Keep in mind when assembling longer right and left triangles with shorter center triangles, that there will be excess right and left triangle length at the end of the seams, so you should only worry about matching up ends at the center points of the triangles.

19 With right sides together, using a ½" seam allowance and beginning at the center points, sew the top-center triangle together with the top-left triangle. (Take care not to stretch out these seams when sewing, as the angles are not cut on the grain.) Press the seam open.

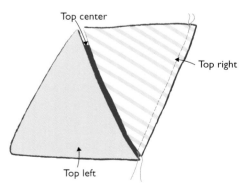

Step 20

20 With right sides together, using a ½" seam allowance and beginning at the center points, sew the top-right triangle together with the joined top center and left triangles. Press the seam open.

21 Repeat Steps 19 and 20 with the bottom three triangles.

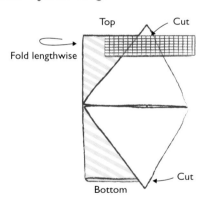

Step 22

22 With right sides together and using a ½" seam allowance, sew the joined top triangles with the joined bottom triangles in one horizontal seam, making sure that the center points match up. Press the seam open.

Trim the Quilt Top

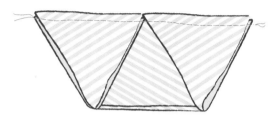

Step 23

23 Fold the quilt top right sides together in half lengthwise, thereby meeting right and left hexagon points. With the help of the quilt ruler, trim off the top excess points horizontally, to be in line with the top edge. Repeat at the bottom edge.

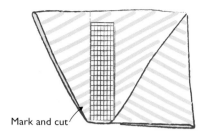

Mark and cut

Step 24

24 Keeping the quilt top folded vertically, fold it again crosswise (on the center horizontal seam) so that you are aligning the top and bottom edges. Lay the corner of the quilt ruler at the bottom left where all the outer corners meet. Begin marking a vertical line with fabric chalk, starting at the outer corner point and continuing up to the crosswise fold. (While the quilt ruler is used to make sure that the vertical line is perpendicular to the top/bottom edges, you can switch to a yardstick once you get the line established.)

25 Cut on the vertical line through all layers, using a yardstick for stability if necessary. Set the pieced scraps aside.

Assemble the Quilt Layers

26 After taking a final measurement of your finished quilt top, you can cut the backing piece in a size to exceed these dimensions by a few inches on all sides. For instance, if the final quilt top measurement is 38" × 53", it might be a good idea to use the full width of a 44/45" fabric to accommodate the 38" measurement, and then cut the backing length at about 60" to accommodate the 53" measurement.

27 Secure a clean, smooth surface, such as a large counter, table, or the floor. Lay the backing out so that the wrong side is facing up. Use some masking tape to tape down the corners and a few spots along all edges to keep the backing smooth and square, but don't stretch it out too tightly.

28 Lay a single, smooth layer of the quilt batting onto the wrong side of the backing, and trim off the excess batting around all edges to make it the same size as the backing.

29 Layer the quilt top over the batting wrong side down, centered within the larger size of the batting and backing. Smooth the quilt top out well. Starting at the center, begin pinning through all three layers using the quilting safety pins, and work your way out. Placing safety pins about every 8" or so in both directions is ideal.

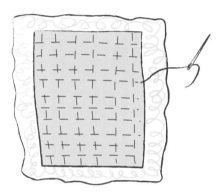

Step 30

30 Once you're finished pinning, you can remove the masking tape holding down the backing. Use a large hand-basting needle and thread to make several rows of long-running basting stitches in both directions through all three layers (when I say long stitches, even an inch or so would be fine). Spacing the rows about 6–8" apart is suitable. It's also a good idea to baste the outer perimeter about ¼" away from the edge of the quilt top. Remove the safety pins. (Keep in mind that if the safety pins won't get in the way for your particular desired quilting method, then you can leave the pins in place.)

Stitch the Quilt: A Few Words About Hand-Quilting Methods

NOTE: At this juncture, you may choose to hand the quilt over to a professional for machine or hand-quilting to stitch all the layers together. If so, be sure to ask whether they will also be binding the quilt and how much fabric they require for this. If you are just going to be binding the quilt yourself, skip to Step 31. Follow the next steps if you'd like to do some hand-quilting yourself.

Decide on a Quilting Pattern

I chose to first simply follow the long seams between the triangles to create a charming and graphic asterisk design over the whole quilt. My stitches are simple, running quilt stitches about ¼" long, and rest ¼" away from each side of the seam. I also randomly selected a few of the seams between strips in each triangle to quilt, which adds a little more dimension and helps along the hexagonal shape. Be sure to consider how the quilting will look on the backing side, too, where it is typically more noticeable. If you are simply following seam lines, then there is no need to mark your stitch pattern. However, if you'd like to make stitches in an unrelated pattern or using a template

of some sort, you'll need to mark the quilt with fabric chalk, pencil, or a water-soluble marker.

Needle and Thread

Typically, the smaller the stitch, the less thick you want your thread to be. If you'd like to make very small, close together, short stitches, you may choose to go with thinner thread straight from a hand-quilting, 100-percent cotton spool. I really like the look of larger stitches with thicker thread (not to mention that it's quicker to work), so I used DMC's Perle Cotton 5. However, to use these thicker threads, you'll want to use an embroidery needle, which is still nice and sharp like a hand-quilting needle, but has a large enough eye to accommodate the thread thickness.

The Stitch

You shouldn't be able to see any knots from the outside of the quilt, either the top or the back, so you'll need to hide them. To do this, knot the thread within ¼" to ½" of the end of the thread, and trim the end if necessary. Insert the needle into the quilt top just about ½" away from where you will begin your first stitch. Do not, however, push the needle through to the back, but instead come up where you want to begin stitching. You can then pull the needle and thread through until the knot is at the surface. Place your fingers on the end of the pulled-through thread slack and tug until the knot pops underneath the top layer. The knot will then be hidden in the inner layers and not visible from either side.

The goal of the simple running stitch is that it is generally straight and that each stitch is equal in length, equally spaced from other stitches, and equal in its distance from a seam if you are following along side seams. With practice, you will be able to load a few stitches onto the needle at once, in a sort of rocking motion, and then pull through all the stitches at once. While this is efficient, use whatever method gives you the prettiest stitch for now. Enter the quilt top with the needle at a perfect vertical angle, and then as soon as you feel the needle from underneath, angle the needle back up as close to a vertical line as you can to pull it through. Focusing on this motion will help keep the stitches on the underside consistent with those on the quilt top.

Many sewers like to use a quilting hoop or frame to keep all the layers nice and smooth as they stitch. I have a square frame that is made from plastic tubing that I find more useful than a round or oval frame that is harder to make use of once you get to the corners. Whether you use a frame or not, you should always start at the center and work your way out with the quilt stitches. Stitching will be easier with a frame if you don't tighten the fabrics so much that you can't press gently on the quilt layer. Also, stop stitching about an inch or two from the inside edges of the frame to prevent skewing the layers at all. Rather, continue to reposition the frame once you get that close.

To make a finishing knot, the concept is similar to the beginning knot. When you are about to perform your last stitch into the quilt top, knot the ending slack of your thread about $\frac{1}{4}$" from the quilt top. Insert the needle to finish the stitch, but just through the top and then back out the top again an inch or so away. Pull until the knot is lying against the top. Tug and pop the knot into the batting layer. Cut the thread close to the top, being careful not to clip the quilt top in the process.

Quilt Binding

31 For a finished binding that is $\frac{7}{8}$" wide, you'll need to cut the bias strips $4\frac{1}{2}$" wide. Measure the perimeter of your quilt. Cut and join as many bias strips as necessary to go around the entire perimeter of your quilt, plus about 18".

32 At one end of the bias that is cut at a 45-degree angle, fold back about $\frac{1}{2}$" toward the wrong side and press a crease.

33 Fold and press the bias strip in half lengthwise throughout the entire length to form a nice crease.

34 On the top of the quilt, and starting in the middle of any side of the quilt, lay a bias strip down, lining up the raw edges of the binding with the raw edges of your quilt. Begin sewing through all layers about 10" or 11" from the end of the binding at a $\frac{1}{4}$" seam allowance.

35 Continue sewing and stop $\frac{1}{4}$" away from the corner edge. Fold the binding at a right angle away from the quilt

and form an angled fold. Then fold back down toward the quilt again the opposite way, forming a fold in line with the sewn edge of the quilt. Pin or hold in place.

36 Begin sewing again down the next edge, starting at the edge of the fold of the binding and the edge of the quilt.

37 Repeat Steps 35 and 36 on the other three corners of the quilt.

38 Stop sewing when you are about 12" away from where you began sewing the binding to the quilt.

39 Open the fold of the pressed end of the binding that you began with. Lay the other end of the binding inside the fold of the first.

40 Cut the end of the binding that is lying inside the other at a 45-degree angle that is opposite from the pressed binding's angle, an inch or two away from the pressed binding's edge.

41 Fold the pressed binding back up to smoothly encase the cut one, and pin all layers in place. Finish sewing through all layers at a $\frac{1}{4}$" seam allowance to join the stopping and starting points of your sewing. (You can go back and blind-sew this overlapping joint together when you do the finishing stitching.)

42 Turn the binding up toward the edge of the quilt and press. Then fold down onto the back side just enough to cover your stitching line. Pin in place.

43 At the corners, you'll notice when you turn your binding up toward the edge that a nice mitered corner has been formed. You can also create this same mitered corner on the back side. With the back of the quilt facing you, fold down the binding to cover the stitch line and smooth this fold all the way beyond the edge of the quilt. This will make the binding form an angled fold at the corner. Simply turn this angle back in toward the quilt to cover the next perpendicular side's stitching, and you will have formed the mitered corner. Pin in place.

44 Finish binding on the back side by making an invisible stitch by hand.

Index